I0406832

Dedication

To the healthcare trailblazers who've occasionally swapped stethoscopes for crystal balls, and to the spirited futurists who, while they haven't built a time machine (yet!), are always a step ahead, envisioning what's next.

Your blend of expertise, creativity, and a pinch of audacity has turned conventional healthcare on its head. In an age where the line between medicine and miracles gets blurry, you've managed to make scrubs and lab coats symbols of both care and innovation.

Here's to the future of healthcare – and to all of you who are writing its prescription. Keep leading the way; we're eager to see where you'll take us next!

Introduction

The age-old adage that "change is the only constant" has never rung truer than in today's healthcare sector. With each passing day, as the heartbeats of countless patients echo in hospital corridors, the very pulse of the healthcare industry is evolving, adapting to the rhythm of our rapidly changing world.

At its core, healthcare has always been about tending to the vulnerable, healing the sick, and innovating for better solutions. Historically, the industry has remained somewhat sheltered, immune to the rapid fluctuations of consumer markets. However, the 21st century brought with it a digital revolution that even the most traditional sectors can't ignore.

In the midst of technological breakthroughs and societal shifts, healthcare finds itself at a crossroads. On one side lies the trodden path of conventional care delivery, with its comforting familiarity and entrenched systems. On the other, there's a horizon filled with possibilities: from AI-assisted diagnostics to digital health records, from telemedicine to genome editing. Beyond the tools and technologies, a deeper transformation brews – a shift in how healthcare professionals work, collaborate, and contribute to this sacred endeavor.

This metamorphosis isn't unique to healthcare. Across industries, the notion of 'work' is being deconstructed and redefined. Gone are the days when a career meant clocking in at 9 and leaving at 5, with the same company logo on your paychecks for decades. The modern professional landscape boasts a kaleidoscope of options: remote work, flexible hours, freelancing gigs, and more.

Technology has been the great enabler here, blurring geographical boundaries and tearing down logistical barriers. But it's also a reflection of a deeper societal shift, a newfound appreciation for work-life balance, individual agency, and the need for continuous learning and adaptation.

So, what does this mean for healthcare? An industry that, by its very nature, demands immediacy, presence, and a human touch. How can it reconcile its core principles with these emerging work trends? And more importantly, how can healthcare leaders navigate this complex landscape, ensuring both quality care and the well-being of its professionals?

In the pages that follow, we will delve deep into these questions, exploring the challenges, opportunities, and groundbreaking changes that lie ahead. This book aims to provide a comprehensive understanding of the future of work in healthcare and, perhaps, offer a roadmap for those ready to embark on this exciting journey.

Chapter 1: Overview of the Current State of the Healthcare Sector

The roots of modern healthcare delve deep into the annals of history, reflecting the evolving understanding of human health and wellness. In ancient times, cultures worldwide displayed an innate grasp of the body and the natural world. Remedies were often sought in immediate environments, with spiritual beliefs intricately woven with practical observations. Whether it was Ayurvedic practices in India or the shamanistic rituals of indigenous tribes, healthcare was perceived as an elegant interplay of science, art, and faith.

Sanatoriums of bygone civilizations weren't just healing centers; they stood as monumental symbols of societal achievement. The Greeks constructed Asclepeia, temples exclusively dedicated to the art of healing where both spiritual rites and medical treatments were offered. Meanwhile, ancient China birthed intricate systems of acupuncture and herbal medicine, and the Egyptians demonstrated prowess in surgical methodologies, heralding the dawn of medical specializations.

The Middle Ages saw an evolutionary shift in healthcare paradigms. Grand hospitals and infirmaries emerged, often with strong ties to religious establishments, to cater to the masses. The European monastic infirmaries, for instance, not only provided care but also emerged as focal points for medical research and learning. With advancements in medical understanding, roles within the healthcare sector became more specialized and defined. Physicians were perceived as the torchbearers of diagnosis and treatment, guiding the healthcare journey. Nurses, transitioning from their monastic roles, embodied care and nurturing, overseeing patients' daily needs and supporting physicians. Auxiliary staff, including the likes of apothecaries, became crucial in the medicinal world, preparing drugs and upholding health records.

This established hierarchy brought method to the madness. A systematic approach to healthcare was instituted, where each role had its designated responsibility, ensuring seamless patient care. However, this structure also introduced certain rigidities. Decisions were often top-down, predominantly physician-driven, with limited scope for collaborative or patient-centered care. The concept of hospitals, as central to healthcare as we understand today, evolved over this period. From mere shelters for the sick, they transitioned to comprehensive care hubs, equipped with specialized wards, state-of-the-art equipment, and a gamut of trained professionals. The rise of urban centers and cities further underlined the importance of these centralized healthcare establishments.

Tracing this transformative journey, from the primal instincts of our ancestors to the structured institutions of today, we are reminded of the enduring spirit of human resilience and innovation. It sets the stage, enabling us to understand and appreciate the forthcoming tectonic shifts in the healthcare landscape.

The Digitalization of Healthcare

The digital age, with its whirlwind of innovations, transformed almost every facet of our lives. Industries across the board experienced upheavals, and healthcare was no exception. As computers grew more powerful and the internet more pervasive, a new chapter began in the annals of medical history. Electronic Health Records (EHR) heralded the onset of this digital revolution in healthcare. The cumbersome, often illegible, handwritten notes that physicians and nurses painstakingly created were supplanted by sleek, digital interfaces. These systems not only streamlined record-keeping but also minimized human errors, allowing for improved patient care. With a few clicks, medical professionals could pull up comprehensive patient histories, ensuring that care was both timely and informed.

In tandem with digitized records, there came a surge in advanced imaging and diagnostic technologies. MRI machines, CT scanners, and other advanced modalities painted clearer pictures of the human body than ever before. Diseases that once lurked undetected could now be visualized with striking clarity. Procedures became less invasive, and diagnostic accuracy improved, ensuring patients received more targeted and effective treatments.

Yet, as with any change, this digital influx was met with skepticism and resistance. The older generation of healthcare professionals, accustomed to traditional methods, found it challenging to navigate the new systems. Concerns about data privacy, potential technology glitches, and the impersonal nature of digital interactions were rife. Training sessions were mandatory, and many professionals grumbled about the "unnecessary complications" these digital tools introduced. But over time, as the merits of the digital transformation became increasingly evident, even the staunchest skeptics began to see its value. Improved patient outcomes, efficiency in treatments, and reductions in medical errors gradually turned the tide in favor of embracing the digital future.

Beyond the realm of medical machinery and software, the digital age had another profound impact: it democratized information. No longer were patients solely reliant on their physicians for medical knowledge. Search engines, health forums, and medical databases allowed patients to research symptoms, treatments, and medicines. This newfound accessibility to information empowered patients. They arrived at doctors' clinics with printouts, questions, and a keen desire to understand and participate in their healthcare journey.

This shift was transformative. The doctor-patient relationship began to evolve from a traditionally one-sided dialogue to a more collaborative partnership. Informed patients demanded clearer explanations, sought second opinions, and were more proactive in managing their health.

The digital age didn't just introduce new tools to the healthcare sector; it reshaped the very ethos of care. As we progressed further into this digital realm, it became evident that healthcare's future would be a blend of cutting-edge technology and renewed human connection, with patients at its heart. The march of progress in healthcare, as profound as it has been, hasn't erased the age-old complexities that the sector faces. In fact, in many instances, the advancements have brought to light deeper issues that lurk within the very structures of global healthcare systems.

Welcome to the 21st Century

One of the most pressing concerns for modern healthcare is the sheer volume of demand. As of the 21st century, the world's population has witnessed an explosive growth, with billions seeking medical attention in one form or another. This burgeoning populace isn't just growing; it's aging. With advancements in medical science, people are living longer than ever before. While this increased longevity is a testament to medical successes, it also means a higher prevalence of age-related ailments. Healthcare systems worldwide find themselves stretched thin, trying to cater to the needs of an older, more disease-prone demographic.

The spectrum of prevalent diseases has also shifted. While infectious diseases remain a challenge, especially in developing nations, there's a rising tide of Non-Communicable Diseases (NCDs) that are sweeping across both developed and developing nations. Diabetes, with its sugar-laden grip, is more prevalent than ever, thanks in part to changing lifestyles and dietary habits. Cardiovascular diseases, spurred by sedentary lifestyles, stress, and dietary choices, claim millions of lives annually. Furthermore, the silent epidemic of mental health disorders, once relegated to hushed conversations, has come to the forefront, demanding attention, understanding, and comprehensive care solutions.

While these health challenges mount, the disparity in healthcare access casts a long, often disheartening shadow. The bright lights of metropolitan cities around the world often shine on state-of-the-art hospitals equipped with the latest in medical technology. Patients in these urban areas have a plethora of choices, from specialists to advanced treatments. Contrast this with the rural landscapes, where even basic medical facilities can be miles away, and the picture becomes grim. Rural residents, often with limited resources, find themselves battling not just diseases but also systemic neglect.

This rural-urban divide is just one facet of the disparity. The chasm of inequality is also deeply economic. Wealthier nations, with their robust economies, can invest more in healthcare, research, and infrastructure. Meanwhile, countries with fewer economic resources grapple with outdated facilities, limited medical personnel, and a lack of essential medicines. Even within prosperous nations, economic disparities create tiers of healthcare access, where the affluent receive premium care, and the economically disadvantaged are left to navigate overstretched public healthcare systems.

These complexities are not just challenges; they are urgent calls to action. As the world moves forward, with technology and knowledge at its disposal, the true measure of progress in healthcare will be how effectively it bridges these gaps, ensuring that every individual, regardless of geography or economic status, receives the care they deserve.

Healthcare at the Nexus of Health Delivery

The landscape of healthcare has transformed from being an isolated domain, predominantly steered by medical professionals, into a multifaceted arena influenced by a myriad of sectors. This confluence, while unexpected to some, is a natural evolution as the world becomes more interconnected and interdisciplinary.

The technology sector's foray into healthcare has perhaps been the most palpable and transformative. Tech behemoths, often with no prior healthcare footprint, are now deeply invested in reshaping the future of medicine. Take Artificial Intelligence (AI), for instance. Algorithms capable of parsing vast amounts of data are being harnessed to provide diagnostic insights, sometimes with accuracy surpassing human experts. Machine Learning (ML) models assist in predicting patient outcomes, optimizing treatment pathways, and even forecasting disease outbreaks.

Wearable technology, too, has shifted from being mere fitness trackers to potent health monitors. Devices that track heart rhythms, blood oxygen levels, or even sleep patterns give users real-time insights into their health. This constant monitoring not only aids individuals in making informed lifestyle choices but also allows medical professionals to have a more holistic view of a patient's health over time.

Personalized medicine, enabled by advances in genomics and data analytics, stands as another testament to technology's imprint on healthcare. Treatments tailored to an individual's genetic makeup are no longer the stuff of science fiction but are gradually becoming the gold standard in areas like oncology.

Pharmaceutical industries, traditionally seen as the giants of healthcare, have begun to tap into the expertise of the financial sector. The development of new drugs, especially those targeting rare or complex conditions, requires vast sums of investment.

Collaborations with financial institutions and investment banks help streamline the funding process, ensuring that promising drug candidates don't falter due to a lack of resources.

The real estate sector's involvement might seem the most tangential, but upon closer inspection, its contribution is paramount. With the rising demand for specialized healthcare facilities, be it rehab centers, memory care units for dementia patients, or even state-of-the-art surgical centers, the real estate industry is stepping up. Their expertise in developing infrastructure tailored to specific needs ensures that healthcare facilities are not just functional, but also conducive to healing. This involves understanding patient needs, the flow of medical services, and even creating spaces that can adapt to rapidly evolving medical technologies.

The healthcare landscape, when viewed from this prism, appears less like a standalone entity and more like a nexus, with threads connecting it to almost every major industry. This interdependence, rather than diluting the essence of healthcare, enriches it, bringing in diverse perspectives, expertise, and solutions. As we navigate the complexities of modern healthcare, these collaborations and intersections will be pivotal in shaping a future that's both inclusive and innovative.

On Being Patient Centered

The story of healthcare, while steeped in advances and challenges, can never be fully understood without centering its most vital character: the patient. Over the years, this protagonist's role has undergone a significant transformation, shaping and being shaped by the ever-evolving tapestry of healthcare.

In the early days of medical practice, the patient was often seen more as a subject – someone to be treated, often with a limited understanding of their ailment or the prescribed remedies.

Information flowed one way: from the doctor to the patient. However, as we entered the age of digital democratization, this traditional dynamic began to shift.

Today, the patient stands informed. A fleeting symptom, a newly prescribed medicine, a looming surgery – all of these are immediately thrust into the vast repository of the internet, returning a plethora of articles, studies, personal anecdotes, and more. This instant access to information allows patients to engage in meaningful conversations with their healthcare providers, seeking clarity, weighing options, and making informed decisions.

Online communities and forums play a crucial role in this empowerment. Patients diagnosed with specific conditions often find solace and support in digital groups where experiences, advice, and resources are shared. These platforms allow for a communal understanding and navigating of health challenges, rendering patients less isolated in their experiences.

Then there's the rise of wearables and health apps, turning patients into active monitors of their well-being. Daily steps, sleep cycles, heart rate variations, dietary intakes – these are now routinely tracked, giving patients a comprehensive view of their health landscape. Such insights lead to proactive health decisions, be it tweaking one's diet, adjusting sleep habits, or consulting a specialist for observed anomalies.

With this empowerment comes a heightened expectation. Modern patients are no longer content with just receiving care; they want to co-create it. They seek transparency in treatment plans, costs, and potential outcomes. They demand efficiency in service delivery, minimal wait times, and swift responses. Personalized care, tailored to their unique needs and preferences, is not just a luxury but an expectation.

The digital age has equipped patients with platforms to voice their experiences and feedback. Online reviews, social media shout-outs, and patient satisfaction surveys play a pivotal role in shaping the reputation of healthcare providers. Such feedback, both positive and negative, pushes hospitals, clinics, and practitioners to continuously improve their offerings. In many ways, patients have evolved into vital quality control agents, ensuring that healthcare systems remain accountable and responsive.

The modern patient, armed with information, supported by communities, and driven by a desire for quality, has transitioned from a mere spectator to a critical player on the healthcare stage. Their evolving roles and expectations are not mere trends; they're harbingers of a new era in healthcare. An era where patients are not just at the receiving end of care but are at the very heart of its design, delivery, and evolution. This shift, more than any technology or innovation, is set to define the trajectory of healthcare's future. And as we pivot to subsequent chapters, it's this empowered patient's perspective that will guide our exploration into the future of healthcare.

Chapter 2: A Brief Look at the Changing Work Paradigms Across Industries

The modern era is often termed the 'Age of Disruption'. As we navigated the intricate nuances of healthcare in our initial chapter, it became evident that the sector is in a state of flux, primarily driven by its internal dynamics and advancements. But there's more to the story. Beyond the immediate periphery of healthcare lie monumental shifts in the broader professional world. Changes that, while not inherently medical in nature, have profound implications for how healthcare will be delivered, received, and perceived in the years to come.

Imagine a world where your banker works from a beach in Bali, your education is sourced from multiple online platforms rather than a singular institution, and your car is not owned but accessed as a service. Sounds futuristic? This is the reality many industries are already stepping into, and these changes are not merely operational—they represent a fundamental rethinking of what work is, where it happens, and how it's executed.

It's an intricate dance of technology, socio-cultural evolution, and economic necessities, each playing their part in this great reshuffle of the traditional work model. To grasp the trajectory of healthcare's evolution, we cannot afford to view it in isolation. It's part of this larger narrative, influenced by and influencing the global work metamorphosis.

In this expanded vista, we'll uncover the trends, transitions, and transformations that are redrawing the boundaries of industries. By understanding these broader shifts, we not only gain a panoramic view of the global professional landscape but also equip ourselves with the knowledge to anticipate and navigate the changes awaiting the healthcare sector.

In any epoch of transformation, it is vital to trace back to the origins — to understand the why behind the what. Our current professional realm isn't just undergoing a spontaneous metamorphosis; it's reacting to an array of powerful catalysts. These forces, sometimes overt and at other times subtle, are reshaping the core of how industries operate. Let's dive deep into these instigators of change.

- Technological Revolution: At the forefront of this change is the exponential growth of technology. The digital revolution, powered by the ubiquity of the internet and the proliferation of smart devices, has torn down geographical barriers. Cloud computing, Artificial Intelligence, and Blockchain are not mere buzzwords; they are enablers that are transforming the modus operandi of businesses, from supply chains to customer interactions.

- Socio-cultural Shifts: The values, beliefs, and aspirations of newer generations are significantly different from those of their predecessors. Millennials and Gen Z, having grown up in a digitized world, seek purpose over paycheck, flexibility over rigidity, and experiences over possessions. Their approach to work-life balance, career progression, and organizational loyalty is reshaping corporate cultures globally.

- Economic Tides: The past decades have witnessed economic booms and recessions, each leaving an indelible mark on industry structures. The push towards leaner operations, the advent of shared economies, and the transition from ownership to access are outcomes of evolving economic paradigms and necessities.

- Global Events: Events of global magnitude, whether they're economic crises, political upheavals, or pandemics like COVID-19, act as accelerators of change. The recent pandemic, for instance, expedited the adoption of remote work, showcased the fragility of rigid supply chains, and underscored the need for digital readiness across sectors.

- Environmental Concerns: As our planet grapples with environmental challenges, sustainability has surged to the forefront. Industries are now reassessing their carbon footprints, waste management, and sourcing practices. The drive towards green operations isn't just an ethical choice but is increasingly becoming a competitive necessity.

- Regulatory and Policy Evolutions: Governments and regulatory bodies, in their bid to protect consumers, ensure fair trade, and stimulate economies, constantly tweak policies. These shifts, whether they're data privacy laws, trade tariffs, or labor rights, have direct implications on how industries function and strategize.

In essence, the tapestry of today's work paradigm is woven with threads of technological marvels, evolving human aspirations, economic realities, global events, ecological concerns, and regulatory frameworks. Each of these catalysts, individually and collectively, is compelling industries to rethink, restructure, and reinvent. As we proceed, we'll delve deeper into how these forces manifest in tangible changes, influencing sectors including, but not limited to, healthcare.

The transformational forces we discussed previously are giving rise to tangible shifts in our work dynamics. What's particularly fascinating is that these shifts aren't merely operational tweaks but represent profound evolutions in our understanding of what constitutes "work."

Remote work, once a luxury or an exception, has now entrenched itself as a norm for many. Companies from Silicon Valley stalwarts to emerging startups have embraced this model, making headlines with permanent remote work options. The traditional office setting, with its nine-to-five constraints, is being challenged by professionals working from cafes in Paris, beaches in Bali, or co-working hubs in bustling cities. Beyond tech firms, even sectors like finance and consultancy, are finding merit in the hybrid model, blending traditional office hours with remote flexibility.

Parallel to this is the blossoming of the gig economy. The success of platforms like Uber, Airbnb, and Upwork attests to a changing workforce appetite. Professionals, especially the younger generation, are gravitating towards short-term, flexible contracts instead of the lifelong employment model of yesteryears. This isn't confined to just a few sectors; even core areas like education and healthcare are witnessing the rise of freelancers or contract-based roles.

The Notion of Fixed, Rigid Job Roles is Fading

Companies, in their bid for innovation and adaptability, are encouraging employees to don multiple hats. It's not uncommon to find tech professionals dabbling in design or marketers diving into data analytics. This fluidity augments creativity fosters a holistic understanding of business operations and ensures that companies remain agile. Initiatives by leading firms, like Google's encouragement for employees to spend time on personal projects, have birthed innovations that might have seemed orthogonal to traditional role definitions.

Adding another dimension to this evolving dynamic is the transformation of workspaces. The office isn't just a place to work; it's becoming a space to collaborate, innovate, and rejuvenate. Companies, both big and small, are rethinking their physical spaces. Vibrant co-working spaces are mushrooming across cities, catering to freelancers, startups, and even established giants looking for a change in scenery.

Collectively, these shifts present both challenges and opportunities. They redefine efficiency, challenge management norms, and offer a fresh canvas for innovation. As we delve deeper, we'll explore how these broader trends intersect with the healthcare sector, painting a picture of what the future might hold for medical professionals and institutions.

The Healthcare Industry Isn't Immune

Every industry, while unique in its core functions and challenges, does not exist in isolation. The ripples of change that sweep across the corporate world are bound to wash up on the shores of healthcare, a sector as essential as it is expansive.

The momentum behind remote work translates effortlessly into the realm of telemedicine, where patients and doctors no longer need to share the same physical space for consultations. Just as professionals from various sectors have found value in working away from traditional office environments, healthcare practitioners are discovering that many aspects of patient care can be managed from a distance, without compromising on quality.

The blossoming gig economy has its mirror in healthcare as well. There's a rising cohort of healthcare professionals who prefer contract-based roles, moving from one institution or project to the next. These professionals, much like freelancers in other industries, value flexibility and varied experiences over static, long-term positions. This model also allows healthcare institutions to tap into a vast pool of talent, scaling up or down based on demand and ensuring specialized care when needed.

The trend of role flexibility and skill fluidity aligns with an inter-disciplinary approach in healthcare. We see nutritionists working closely with mental health professionals or data scientists partnering with oncologists to better understand patient data. The barriers between specializations are blurring, leading to a more holistic and patient-centric approach to care.

The transformation of workspaces, while more pronounced in sectors like tech and finance, has lessons for healthcare as well. It's not just about building hospitals or clinics but creating spaces that promote wellness, healing, and collaboration. The future might see more 'healing spaces' integrated within communities, where the focus isn't just on treating illness but promoting overall well-being.

Understanding these parallels is crucial. It gives us a lens to view the healthcare sector not as a monolithic entity resistant to change but as a dynamic field ready to adapt, innovate, and evolve. As we proceed, we'll delve into the nitty-gritty of this transformation, guided by the lessons and trends we've gleaned from the broader corporate landscape. This rich tapestry of insights will shape our exploration of the future of work in healthcare, a journey both exciting and essential.

Chapter 3: A Historical Perspective: Work in Healthcare Then and Now

From the earliest shamans who served as tribal healers to the multidisciplinary teams of today's medical centers, the journey of healthcare work is a testament to humanity's adaptive spirit and undying commitment to wellness. Throughout these ages, healthcare has constantly evolved, intertwining with societal norms, technological progress, and ever-changing challenges.

The 20th century Stands Out

The beginning of the century was marked by the groundbreaking discovery of the X-ray by Wilhelm Conrad Roentgen, which laid the foundation for modern radiology. Following this, medical technology saw a boom with innovations like the electrocardiograph, improvements in surgical techniques, and the introduction of Magnetic Resonance Imaging (MRI) and Computed Tomography (CT) scans. These tools revolutionized diagnostic medicine, allowing clinicians to see inside the human body with unprecedented clarity.

Perhaps one of the most profound developments was the discovery and mass production of antibiotics. Alexander Fleming's serendipitous discovery of penicillin heralded the era of antibiotics, transforming medicine by drastically reducing mortality from bacterial infections. Following this wave, the century saw the development of vaccines for diseases like polio, measles, and mumps, and significant advances in chemotherapy for cancer treatment.

Simultaneously, the 20th century also championed the concept of evidence-based medicine. Medical practices began to shift away from anecdotes and toward treatments and procedures rooted in rigorous scientific research. Clinical trials became standardized, ensuring that new treatments were both safe and effective.

The complexity of medicine led to the emergence of various specialties. From cardiologists focusing on heart health to radiologists interpreting medical images, the spectrum of specialized roles expanded dramatically. This led to a profound change in patient care, wherein physicians, surgeons, nurses, pharmacists, and other healthcare professionals began to collaborate, offering comprehensive care.

On the global front, the post-war period recognized the necessity for coordinated efforts to address worldwide health challenges. This realization culminated in the establishment of the World Health Organization, which became instrumental in addressing global health crises, setting health standards, and driving initiatives like the eradication of smallpox.

As medical treatments advanced and became costlier, the need for robust healthcare systems and insurance models became evident. Countries like the UK saw the inception of the National Health Service, aiming to provide healthcare for all. Meanwhile, in the US, Medicare and Medicaid emerged in the 1960s to aid the elderly and the poor.

With these advancements came challenges, leading to a deeper understanding of medical ethics. The latter half of the century saw an emphasis on patient rights, informed consent, and ethical considerations in medical research.

The 20th century was not just about technological and pharmaceutical advancements but also about reimagining the ethos of healthcare, ensuring that it remained scientific, ethical, and patient-centric.

Ancient Civilizations and Healthcare:

In the annals of ancient civilizations, from Mesopotamia to Indus Valley, healthcare was deeply entwined with spirituality. The earliest health practitioners were often priests or revered community members. For instance, Imhotep in ancient Egypt was not only a vizier and high priest but is also considered one of the earliest physicians. They combined their understanding of herbs, natural remedies, and the human body with spiritual rituals to treat ailments. In ancient China, traditional medicine like acupuncture began, based on the balance of forces - yin and yang.

Medieval Period:

As societies transitioned into the medieval age, there was a mix of progress and regression in healthcare. While the Islamic world saw the rise of scholars like Ibn Sina (Avicenna) who penned the 'Canon of Medicine', Europe grappled with challenges like the Bubonic Plague. Monastic infirmaries were the precursors to hospitals, but the majority of care happened at home. This was also a period when the roles of midwives and barber-surgeons became distinct.

Renaissance and Enlightenment:

The Renaissance marked a turning point. With the advent of the printing press, medical knowledge became more widespread. The period also witnessed the birth of medical illustrations, exemplified by Andreas Vesalius's 'De Humani Corporis Fabrica'. The Enlightenment further propelled this progress with a more rigorous approach to science and empiricism.

The Industrial Revolution:

The rapid urbanization during the Industrial Revolution posed new public health challenges - overcrowding, poor sanitation, and the spread of infectious diseases. This led to the birth of roles like the 'sanitary inspector'. The establishment of formal medical schools and the push for evidence-based medicine (like the work of John Snow in epidemiology) started shaping modern medical practice.

20th Century Advancements:

The 1900s marked a series of transformative changes. The discovery of the X-ray by Wilhelm Conrad Roentgen, the development of antibiotics, and the foundation of evidence-based practice started redefining patient care. The rise of specialized roles - from cardiologists to radiologists - meant that patient care became a concerted effort of various experts. Furthermore, the establishment of organizations like the World Health Organization in 1948 signified a global, unified approach to health challenges.

The Digital Age:

The last few decades, characterized by rapid technological advancements, have further morphed healthcare. Electronic Health Records (EHRs), Machine Learning in diagnostics, telemedicine platforms, and patient portals have redefined the patient-care provider relationship. The roles too have evolved, with the emergence of health IT specialists, genetic counselors, and more.

The Digital Age: Unprecedented Change

The transition into the Digital Age has brought about profound transformations in the realm of healthcare. The introduction of Electronic Health Records (EHRs) marked a significant departure from paper-based patient histories and treatment logs. These digital records streamlined patient data management, allowing for more accurate diagnoses, tracking of treatment outcomes, and improved coordination among care providers.

Machine Learning, an offshoot of artificial intelligence, began making its mark in diagnostics. By analyzing vast datasets, these algorithms can assist doctors in detecting diseases, predicting patient outcomes, and even suggesting potential treatment paths with greater accuracy and speed than traditional methods. This symbiosis between man and machine augments the clinician's expertise, offering insights drawn from data patterns that might be too subtle for the human eye.

Telemedicine platforms, bolstered by improved internet connectivity, have democratized healthcare access. No longer were consultations limited by geographical constraints. A patient in a remote village could now connect with a specialist in a metropolitan center, ensuring timely and expert care. These platforms have been especially crucial in bridging the healthcare gap in underserved regions, making specialized medical advice more universally accessible.

In tandem with these changes, patient portals emerged, placing patients firmly at the center of their healthcare journey. These digital platforms grant patients access to their medical histories, laboratory results, and appointment schedules. Furthermore, they empower patients with the tools to take a proactive role in their health, from setting up appointments to seeking clarifications on their conditions.

With the digitization of healthcare came the need for professional that are adept at bridging the gap between medicine and technology. Health IT specialists emerged as the unsung heroes, ensuring the seamless integration of technological solutions into everyday medical practice. Moreover, as our understanding of genetics deepened and became more accessible, the role of genetic counselors became prominent. These experts guide patients through the complex world of genetic testing, interpreting results, and advising on potential health implications.

The Digital Age has not just introduced new tools and platforms; it has reshaped the very essence of healthcare. The dynamic has shifted from a predominantly reactive model to a proactive, collaborative, and patient-centric one. With technology as the catalyst, healthcare today is more data-driven, personalized, and accessible than ever before.

Today, as we stand at the precipice of the digital age, healthcare is experiencing yet another metamorphosis. Digital technologies, telemedicine, and data analytics are reshaping the way professionals collaborate, how care is delivered, and how patients engage in their health journeys. Each period in history has added a layer, be it in terms of roles, technologies, or methodologies. This layered evolution tells a story — a story of resilience, innovation, and an undying commitment to the betterment of human health. As we delve deeper into the subsequent sections, we'll unpack these layers, drawing insights from the past to inform the future.

Chapter 4: Traditional Roles in Healthcare and the Hierarchical Structure

In exploring the annals of healthcare, one observes a pronounced hierarchical system—a relic of an era when structure and specialization were paramount to effective care. This approach, while advantageous in many respects, was a double-edged sword, shaping both the efficiency and the limitations of healthcare delivery.

The Physicians Role

The role of a physician has always been one of prestige and responsibility. Historically, they were often seen as the bridge between the mystical and the mundane, wielding the knowledge to both diagnose and treat, armed with a mix of science and intuition.

To truly understand the elevated position of physicians, it's essential to look back in history. In ancient civilizations, those who practiced medicine were often aligned with the divine. They were the chosen ones, trusted with not only physical but spiritual well-being. This sanctified position gradually evolved as the intersection of science and medicine became more pronounced. By the time of the Renaissance and Enlightenment, the physician was the educated scholar, merging empirical observation with methodical study.

The journey to becoming a physician has always been rigorous. The lengthy educational requirements—often spanning over a decade—combined with grueling residencies and specializations, ensured that by the time physicians were ready to practice, they had a depth of expertise unrivaled by most other professions. This extensive training not only equipped them with vast medical knowledge but also honed their critical thinking and decision-making skills.

With such formidable training and knowledge, physicians naturally assumed the role of the primary decision-makers in the healthcare setting. Their diagnoses set the tone for a patient's therapeutic journey. Their expertise influenced everything from medication choices to surgical interventions. In many ways, the physician was the captain of the ship, guiding it through the turbulent seas of illness and towards the shores of recovery.

Yet, with great power came great responsibility—and often, immense pressure. Being at the helm meant physicians bore the brunt of challenges, from navigating complex cases to managing patient expectations. Moreover, the very nature of their elevated status sometimes created barriers. It occasionally distanced them from the collaborative ethos that modern healthcare is evolving towards. The traditional model of the all-knowing physician had its benefits, but as healthcare advanced and became more multifaceted, the need for interprofessional collaboration grew.

While physicians have historically been at the forefront of healthcare decision-making—and continue to play a pivotal role—the evolving landscape of healthcare demands a shift. A shift from solitary decision-making to collaborative strategizing, ensuring the best outcomes for patients in an increasingly complex medical world.

The Healthcare Team

The multifaceted world of healthcare is akin to a symphony—each player crucial, each note essential. If physicians were the conductors, guiding the flow and pace, then the myriad other professionals were the orchestra, creating the harmony and depth that brought the performance to life.

Nurses, in particular, have been instrumental in healthcare's evolution. They donned multiple hats—from caregivers to educators, advocates to confidantes. It's a profession built on empathy and grit, requiring both clinical acumen and unparalleled human touch. Throughout history, nurses have often been the first point of contact for patients, and their continuous presence on the frontline has been pivotal in shaping positive patient outcomes.

While the image of a pharmacist might conjure a professional behind a counter, their impact extends far beyond. Historically, they've been the custodians of medicinal knowledge—understanding not just the properties of drugs, but also their interactions, side effects, and optimal dosages. In many healthcare settings, they act as a bridge between the diagnosing physician and the patient, clarifying doubts, ensuring adherence, and flagging potential concerns.

There's the vast array of auxiliary professionals, each specializing in their domain yet interconnected in the grander scheme of patient care. Lab technicians, with their precise skills, ensure that every sample is treated with utmost care, delivering results that inform critical clinical decisions. Radiologists dive deep into the world of imaging, unraveling the mysteries that lie beneath the skin. Therapists, be it physical, occupational, or speech, bring a specialized skill set, helping patients navigate the complexities of recovery or adaptation.

These professionals form the intricate tapestry of healthcare. Their roles, while distinct, are interconnected, reinforcing the idea that healthcare, at its core, is a collaborative endeavor. In the face of ever-evolving challenges and medical advancements, these professionals adapt, learn, and continue to play their part in delivering holistic care to those in need.

This well-choreographed dance of roles worked in harmony, largely due to the clarity the hierarchy provided. Decisions made at the top trickled down, ensuring a uniform approach to care. Yet, this system was not without its flaws. The top-down structure, while fostering respect for expertise, often stifled voices from the "lower" ranks. Many a time, nurses or technicians with valuable insights or on-ground observations found it challenging to challenge or influence the decision-making process. Collaboration was present but often limited by the rigid boundaries of the hierarchy.

The siloed nature of these roles sometimes led to fragmented care. While each professional was adept at their specific role, there were instances where a more integrated, holistic approach might have been beneficial for the patient. The question of inclusivity, both in terms of roles and gender (with certain roles traditionally dominated by one gender), also loomed large.

While the traditional hierarchical structure in healthcare had its merits, fostering efficiency and clear delineation of roles, it also posed challenges, particularly in terms of inclusivity, collaboration, and holistic patient care. As the winds of change blew, the need for a more integrated, collaborative, and patient-centric model became increasingly evident.

Hierarchy in Healthcare

Healthcare, for much of its history, again functioned like a well-tuned orchestra. Each professional played their part, and the melodies, for the most part, resonated well. The clearly defined hierarchies and role demarcations ensured that everyone knew their position and responsibilities. Such a structure was invaluable in maintaining order, especially in high-stress situations where ambiguity could be detrimental. A physician's decision, backed by years of study and experience, was rarely questioned. Nurses, pharmacists, and technicians, with their specialized expertise, ensured the seamless execution of these decisions.

But, like any system, it had its nuances. Imagine, for a moment, an orchestra where only the conductor's viewpoint is considered, and the individual musicians' insights—born out of their unique relationship with their instruments—are overlooked. The result might still be a melody, but perhaps not as rich or as attuned to the subtleties of the performance.

In the same vein, while physicians were adept at diagnosis and treatment planning, the on-ground realities, often observed by nurses or technicians, were invaluable. These professionals, closer to the patients, sometimes picked up nuances that could be crucial to care—be it a patient's non-verbal cues, their emotional state, or even subtle physical reactions. The hierarchical structure, in its rigidity, sometimes overshadowed these insights, potentially leading to missed opportunities for enhanced care.

The distinct compartments within which professionals operated meant that while each was a master of their domain, they often worked in isolation. This could lead to fragmented care, where the whole might not always equal the sum of its parts. A technician's observation, a nurse's intuition, or a pharmacist's suggestion, when integrated, could offer a richer, more nuanced perspective on patient care.

The world of healthcare wasn't immune to societal structures and biases. Historically, certain roles within healthcare were gendered. For instance, nursing was often seen as a predominantly female profession, while surgery was male dominated. Such demarcations, while reflective of the times, posed questions of representation and equity.

Looking back, it's evident that while the hierarchical, compartmentalized approach served its purpose in providing structured care, it also had its limitations. As the broader world began to evolve, valuing collaboration and integration, so too did the whispers within the hallowed halls of healthcare. The clamor grew louder for a model that was more inclusive, valuing the voices of all professionals, and centering care around the patient's holistic well-being.

The Shifting Paradigm

The age of digital medicine has reimagined what it means to practice healthcare. Previously, the confines of physical walls dictated the reach of healthcare professionals. A clinic or a hospital was more than just a place; it was an emblem of care, a sanctuary of healing. But as technology advanced, these walls began to dissolve, replaced by digital bridges connecting professionals to patients, regardless of geography.

Telemedicine emerged as a beacon of hope for many who had previously faced insurmountable barriers to care. Imagine a patient in a remote village, miles away from the nearest medical facility, now being able to consult with a specialist in a metropolitan city. Or consider the chronically ill elderly individual, for whom frequent hospital visits are both cumbersome and exhausting, now being monitored and consulted from the comfort of their homes. These scenarios, once a mere figment of imagination, became realities.

The emergence of remote roles had a profound impact on collaborative care. Complex cases could now be discussed in virtual multi-disciplinary teams, comprising specialists from across the globe. This meant that patients, irrespective of where they were located, had the potential to access the best minds in medicine.

As with any paradigm shift, challenges accompanied the opportunities. The tactile element of care, the physical touch, the reassuring pat on the back, or the face-to-face conversation – could these be replicated on a screen? Would the warmth of a doctor's demeanor translate through pixels? And beyond the interpersonal aspects, there were practical concerns. How could one ensure the accuracy of remotely collected data? What about the potential pitfalls and vulnerabilities of storing sensitive patient data on digital platforms?

The relationship dynamics began to evolve. Patients, now equipped with digital tools and platforms, began to actively participate, chart, and even monitor their health metrics. This shifted the balance, making them more than just receivers of care, evolving into active participants.

As healthcare professionals navigated these changes, training and adaptability became paramount. Learning to communicate effectively online, ensuring patient comfort, and staying updated with the rapid technological advancements became essential components of the modern healthcare toolkit.

In reflecting upon this transformative journey, it becomes evident that while the medium of care delivery has evolved, the essence remains unaltered. Whether in person or over a screen, the goal remains the same: to heal, to comfort, and to care. The emergence of remote-capable roles is just another chapter in healthcare's ongoing story of adaptation and evolution, ever striving to meet the needs of its most important stakeholder – the patient.

The Patient as Engaged Customer

As the 21st century unfolded, there was a palpable shift in the dynamics of healthcare. The once clear demarcation between the caregiver and the receiver began to blur. The "doctor knows best" approach, while still revered for its expertise, started to be complemented by the "patient knows self" perspective. Patients, with a plethora of health information just a click away, started arriving at clinics and hospitals armed with knowledge, queries, and sometimes even potential diagnoses.

This democratization of health information, spurred by the internet and digital technologies, was a double-edged sword. While it empowered patients, making them informed partners in their health journey, it also posed challenges. Healthcare professionals often found themselves navigating a minefield of misinformation, debunking myths, and recalibrating patient expectations shaped by the vast expanse of the web.

Yet, amidst these challenges lay immense opportunities. The healthcare industry began to realize that an informed patient could be an asset. Engaged patients often adhered better to treatment regimens, were more proactive in managing their health, and actively sought preventive measures. This evolution was not just limited to online resources. Wearable technologies, tracking everything from heart rates to sleep cycles, gave patients real-time data about their bodies, further deepening their engagement with their health.

Consequently, the narrative began to shift. Instead of dictating care pathways, healthcare professionals started to embrace a more collaborative approach. Treatment plans became conversations, with patients sharing their insights, preferences, and apprehensions. This mutual respect and collaboration meant that care became more holistic, considering not just the physical ailment but also the patient's mental and emotional well-being, lifestyle preferences, and long-term goals.

The healthcare environment began to reflect this change. Waiting rooms transformed into spaces of engagement, with interactive screens and educational materials. Hospitals and clinics started hosting patient education sessions, workshops, and support groups, acknowledging and nurturing the patient's role as an active stakeholder.

Reflecting on this journey, it's fascinating to see how the healthcare landscape, so deeply rooted in its traditional hierarchies, has metamorphosed. It's a testament to the sector's adaptability, its inherent commitment to better patient outcomes, and its acknowledgment that in the intricate dance of healthcare, both the professional and the patient have pivotal roles to play. As we forge ahead, this spirit of collaboration and mutual respect promises to be the cornerstone of future healthcare models.

Chapter 5: Remote Work in Healthcare: Beyond Telemedicine

In an age where almost every facet of our lives can be managed through a digital screen, it's no surprise that the healthcare sector has joined the fray. While telemedicine is often the poster child of remote work in healthcare, the shift to remote operations is far more expansive, touching everything from patient care to administrative tasks. Let's explore this landscape, its challenges, and the innovative solutions being crafted in response.

The digital revolution has seeped into myriad corners of our lives, from ordering food to connecting with loved ones across the globe. Healthcare, being an indispensable aspect of human life, has not remained untouched by this wave. The narrative often begins with telemedicine, but in reality, the tendrils of remote work in healthcare extend much further, redefining boundaries and reimagining possibilities.

One could argue that healthcare was always somewhat 'remote'. Home visits by doctors in the past, phone consultations, and even mailed medical results were early hints. But today's remote healthcare is an entirely different beast, bolstered by technology and driven by a blend of necessity and innovation.

For instance, routine consultations, which once required physical presence, have transformed. A doctor in San Francisco can now review a patient's symptoms, assess their condition through a video call, and even prescribe medication to someone in rural Montana. It's not just about bridging distances; it's about increasing efficiency. A dermatologist might see more patients through back-to-back online consultations than they would in a traditional clinic setup, eliminating the downtime that comes with physical appointments.

But it's not just doctors making the shift. A plethora of roles within the healthcare system is becoming remote-compatible. Medical coding, traditionally an office-based role, has seen a shift towards home-based operations, with coders accessing patient records securely from their own desks. Similarly, health education and patient advocacy, crucial in managing chronic illnesses like diabetes or hypertension, have found a home in virtual platforms, with educators reaching out to wider audiences.

Healthcare support roles, too, are undergoing a transformation. IT teams supporting healthcare infrastructure might be dispersed across various locations, ensuring that systems remain operational 24/7. Medical transcriptionists, once staples in hospitals, now often operate from remote locales, transcribing doctor-patient interactions from recordings.

The shift, however, isn't without its complexities. The very essence of healthcare — its deeply personal, often intimate nature — poses questions about the efficacy and ethics of remote operations. Can a psychiatrist effectively counsel a patient over a video call? How do doctors ensure that the patient on the other side of the screen understands the nuances of a diagnosis or a prescribed treatment? And amidst this, looming large are concerns of data privacy and security. Every virtual consultation, every online record entry is a potential point of vulnerability.

There's a concerted effort to enhance security protocols, develop guidelines for remote patient care, and train medical professionals to adapt to this new mode of operation. End-to-end encryption, multi-factor authentication, and stringent data access controls are becoming norms rather than exceptions.

The transition to remote healthcare, much like the broader shift to remote work, is a balancing act — weighing the promise of efficiency and accessibility against challenges of quality, security, and the irreplaceable human touch. As the sector navigates this evolving terrain, one thing is clear: the future of healthcare is not just about new medicines or innovative surgeries; it's also about reimagining where, how, and by whom care is delivered.

Case Studies of Successful Remote Work Adaptations

Case Study 1: Global Radiology Collaboration

Background

Radiology, the branch of medicine that employs medical imaging to diagnose and treat diseases, is a cornerstone of modern healthcare. Historically, the interpretation of these images was constrained by geography. A patient in London, for instance, would typically have their X-rays or MRIs reviewed by a local radiologist, and the scope for a second opinion was limited to the expertise available within a close radius.

The Challenge

With the rise of complex diseases and the increasing sophistication of imaging technologies, the demand for specialized radiologists grew. Certain rare conditions or nuanced interpretations could benefit from a global expert's insights. However, the traditional model was not equipped to quickly tap into this global pool of expertise.

The Shift

Enter the era of digital transformation. With the advent of high-speed internet, secure cloud storage, and advanced data encryption, sharing high-resolution medical images across continents became feasible. Proprietary platforms, dedicated to medical data sharing, began to emerge, promising rapid transmission without compromising patient confidentiality.

The Implementation

A hospital in London, faced with a challenging case, could upload the imaging scans to a secure server. Using a platform interface, they'd send a request to a specialized radiologist in New York, who'd receive a notification. Within minutes, the expert could review the scans, annotate directly on the images, and send back a comprehensive report. The entire process, which earlier could have taken days or even weeks, was now streamlined into hours.

The Benefits

- Speedy Diagnoses: With the ability to tap into global expertise, patient wait times for diagnostic results reduced significantly.
- Enhanced Accuracy: Collaborative reviews meant that challenging cases were assessed from multiple angles, increasing diagnostic accuracy.
- Continual Learning: Local radiologists had the opportunity to engage with global experts, fostering an environment of shared knowledge and continual learning.
- Cost-Efficiency: Transporting patients or experts for second opinions was no longer necessary, resulting in substantial savings.

The Outcome

Patients became the ultimate beneficiaries of this shift. With timely and accurate diagnoses, treatment could commence earlier, improving prognosis. Moreover, the assurance that their cases were being reviewed by some of the best minds in radiology provided an additional layer of confidence.

The Future

While the model has proved successful, the field is continuously evolving. Future developments may include real-time collaborative interpretations, where multiple radiologists from around the world can discuss a case in a virtual conference room. There's also the exciting potential of integrating artificial intelligence to assist in preliminary scans, flagging potential areas of concern for human experts to review.

The Global Radiology Collaboration stands as a testament to the power of technology in bridging geographical divides, reaffirming that in the realm of healthcare, collaboration can save lives.

Case Study 2: Virtual Physical Therapy

Background

Physical therapy plays a crucial role in rehabilitation after injuries, surgeries, or managing chronic conditions. Traditional physical therapy has always necessitated in-person sessions where therapists can guide, correct, and assess a patient's movements. However, frequent visits to clinics might be inconvenient for patients, especially those living in remote areas or having mobility challenges.

The Challenge

How can patients continue their physical therapy regimen without regular in-person sessions, while ensuring that exercises are done correctly? Additionally, how can therapists provide instantaneous feedback from a distance?

The Shift

The convergence of augmented reality (AR) and motion-sensing technologies provided a groundbreaking solution. Instead of relying solely on video calls where nuances of movement might be missed, the integration of AR allowed for a more immersive therapy experience.

The Implementation

Patients, equipped with AR glasses and motion-sensing wearables, could initiate a session from their homes. As they perform their exercises, the motion sensors capture every nuance of their movement. On the therapist's end, a detailed avatar of the patient replicates these movements in real-time. Using AR, the therapist can superimpose correct movement patterns or highlight areas needing correction, which the patient sees through their AR glasses.

For example, if a patient is not bending their knee to the desired angle during a specific exercise, the therapist can overlay a visual cue indicating the correct angle, and the patient can adjust accordingly.

The Benefits

- Accessibility: Patients no longer need to travel for their sessions, making therapy more accessible to a wider demographic.
- Real-Time Feedback: With motion-sensing technologies, therapists can give immediate feedback, ensuring exercises are performed correctly.
- Safety: By ensuring correct postures and movements, the chances of injury during self-practice are significantly reduced.
- Data-Driven Insights: The motion-sensing technology can store data, allowing therapists to track a patient's progress quantitatively.

The Outcome

Patients found the virtual physical therapy sessions to be as effective, if not more, than traditional sessions. They felt empowered to practice on their own with the confidence that they were doing it right. Therapists, on the other hand, could handle more patients and offer flexible timings, thanks to the virtual model.

The Future

The possibilities for growth in virtual physical therapy are immense. Future iterations might include integrating AI to suggest personalized exercise regimes based on a patient's progress, or VR environments where patients can undergo therapy in simulated 'game-like' scenarios, making rehabilitation more engaging. Virtual Physical Therapy represents the innovative blend of technology and healthcare, showcasing that with the right tools, distance is no longer a barrier to effective treatment.

Case Study 3: Remote Patient Monitoring for Chronic Diseases

Background

Chronic diseases like diabetes and cardiac conditions require consistent monitoring. The fluctuations in blood glucose levels for diabetics or the rhythm anomalies in cardiac patients can be indicators of potential complications, necessitating swift medical intervention. Historically, patients would have periodic check-ups at clinics to assess their condition. But what if real-time, continuous monitoring could preempt crises?

The Challenge

Consistent visits to clinics or hospitals for routine monitoring can be strenuous for patients, especially if they have mobility issues or reside in remote areas. Moreover, the period between these visits could miss out on critical anomalies in vital parameters. How can healthcare providers bridge this gap and ensure timely interventions?

The Shift

The fusion of wearable technology with cloud computing provided an answer. Now, patients could be monitored in real-time, regardless of where they were.

The Implementation

Patients were equipped with sleek, user-friendly wearable devices tailored to their specific condition. Diabetics, for instance, had continuous glucose monitoring patches, while cardiac patients sported rhythm monitoring bands or patches. These wearables tracked vital parameters 24/7.

Using encrypted channels, the data was sent to cloud servers in real-time. Here, sophisticated algorithms processed these vast streams of data, searching for patterns or anomalies that might indicate a problem. Should any irregularity be detected, alerts were instantaneously sent to both the healthcare team and the patient.

This system not only facilitated immediate intervention but also collected a rich data set, helping doctors understand disease progression and tailor treatments more effectively.

The Benefits

Proactive Interventions: Instead of waiting for complications to manifest, healthcare providers could act the moment data showed a potential issue.

- Empowering Patients: With continuous feedback, patients could correlate their actions (like food intake or physical activity) with changes in their vitals, fostering better self-management.

- Reducing Hospital Visits: With efficient monitoring from home, the need for routine check-ups diminished, freeing up medical resources and reducing costs.
- Data-Driven Decision Making: The continuous flow of data provided insights that could be used for personalized treatment plans.

The Outcome

Patients embraced the technology, citing peace of mind from the knowledge that they were continuously monitored. Healthcare teams reported quicker response times, potentially averting complications by acting on the data-driven alerts.

The Future

The landscape of remote patient monitoring looks promising, with the potential to integrate AI-driven predictions, offering lifestyle suggestions, medication alterations, or preventive measures based on the collected data. This model demonstrates the power of integrating technology into healthcare, morphing a reactive system into a proactive, patient-centric model.

The Rise of Telemedicine and Its Implications

Telemedicine has democratized access to healthcare, transcending geographical limitations. No longer are specialist consultations restricted to those who live in proximity to large urban centers. This increased access has profound implications:

- Democratized Care: Rural populations, previously underserved, can now access the same caliber of care as their urban counterparts.

- Cost Efficiency: Reducing the need for physical space and resources, telemedicine can potentially lower healthcare costs for providers and patients.

- Continuity of Care: With digital records and virtual follow-ups, continuity of care becomes seamless, enhancing patient outcomes.

However, telemedicine also raises questions about the quality of care, potential misdiagnoses, and the challenges of building rapport with patients remotely.

Remote Administrative Roles and Support Functions

Beyond clinical roles, the healthcare sector has witnessed a surge in remote administrative functions. Medical coders, billers, and even healthcare IT support teams often operate from remote locations. Medical transcription, once confined to the walls of hospitals, is now frequently outsourced to professionals working from their homes or even from different countries. This not only reduces operational costs but also ensures round-the-clock support, given the time zone differences.

Challenges and Solutions to Remote Work

The transition to remote work in healthcare has ushered in numerous benefits, but it also presents certain challenges. Among the primary concerns is data security. As healthcare professionals handle sensitive patient information remotely, the specter of data breaches looms large. To counteract this, advanced measures like end-to-end encryption and secure VPNs are becoming standard practices.

Another significant issue is licensing and regulation. When professionals consult across international boundaries, the complexities of medical licensing come to the fore. Some nations are looking towards establishing unified licensing regimes, while there's also growing advocacy for universal medical licenses. Beyond the logistical challenges, there's the intangible aspect of the human touch. The essence of medicine goes beyond the clinical; it's deeply interpersonal. The physical detachment in remote settings can sometimes create a void in the patient-provider rapport. To address this, emerging technologies such as virtual reality consultations are gaining traction, attempting to replicate the feeling of being physically present.

On the whole, while remote work in healthcare might be seen by some as a modern phenomenon, it's gradually cementing its place as an integral part of the sector's evolution. The road ahead will undoubtedly have its bumps, but with innovation and dedication, healthcare can continue its mission of delivering care that's accessible, effective, and deeply empathetic, regardless of geographical boundaries.

While the shift to remote work in healthcare has been largely positive, it's not without challenges:

- Data Security: Handling sensitive patient information remotely raises concerns about data breaches. Solutions such as end-to-end encryption and secure VPNs are being employed to mitigate these risks.

- Licensing and Regulation: For professionals consulting across borders, navigating the labyrinth of medical licensing becomes complex. Some countries are developing unified licensing systems, while others are advocating for international medical licenses.

- Human Touch: Medicine is as much an art as it is a science. The absence of physical presence can sometimes hinder the patient-provider relationship. Solutions like VR consultations, where patients feel as though they're in the same room as their provider, are being explored to bridge this gap.

Chapter 6: Embracing Flexibility: Part-time, Job Sharing, and More

The traditional 9-to-5 model is becoming less tenable and even less desirable for many healthcare professionals. The dynamics of the industry, coupled with the varied needs of its workforce and the populations they serve, have necessitated a shift in perspective. This chapter delves into the emerging world of flexible work arrangements within healthcare, where the adaptability of roles is paramount.

As healthcare demands increase and the workforce seeks a better balance between their personal and professional lives, flexibility is no longer just an attractive perk—it's a strategic imperative. From the undeniable advantages of flexible working patterns to the innovation of job-sharing roles, we'll explore how these adjustments can lead to enhanced patient care, greater professional satisfaction, and improved retention rates.

It's essential to approach this topic with a balanced lens. While the benefits of such arrangements are numerous, they also present challenges, particularly when ensuring continuity of care and maintaining the sacred patient-provider relationship. By examining real-world examples, evidence-based advantages, and potential pitfalls, we aim to present a comprehensive view of this transformative shift in healthcare employment.

The Advantages of Flexible Working in Healthcare

Flexible working, once a rarity in the strictly regimented world of healthcare, has rapidly gained traction as both healthcare providers and institutions recognize its myriad benefits. This shift in work dynamics has profound implications, benefiting not only the healthcare professionals themselves but also the institutions they serve and, most importantly, the patients under their care.

Enhanced Work-Life Balance: At the forefront of the benefits is the improved work-life balance for healthcare professionals. Balancing the demanding hours of healthcare with personal and familial obligations can lead to burnout. Flexible working allows professionals to tailor their schedules, reducing stress and preventing burnout, leading to improved mental well-being.

Increased Retention and Recruitment: Offering flexible work options makes healthcare roles more attractive to potential candidates. It can also reduce turnover rates, as employees who enjoy a favorable work-life balance are more likely to remain loyal to their employers.

- Optimized Patient Care: Contrary to concerns that flexible working might dilute the quality of care, it often results in more alert, less stressed healthcare professionals. This translates to fewer mistakes, a more patient-centric approach, and improved care outcomes.

- Cost Efficiency: Institutions can manage their staffing costs more effectively by leveraging part-time or flexible roles, especially during peak patient inflows. This dynamic scheduling can lead to significant cost savings without compromising on patient care.

- Reduced Absenteeism: When healthcare professionals have the autonomy to manage their schedules, there's often a marked reduction in absenteeism. Professionals can better manage their health, leading to fewer sick days.

- Accommodating Diverse Needs: Flexible roles can be especially advantageous for those pursuing further education, those with caregiving responsibilities, or those with health issues. This inclusivity ensures a diverse workforce, bringing varied experiences and perspectives to patient care.
- Increased Productivity: A rested, stress-free healthcare worker is invariably more productive. The flexibility allows

professionals to work during their peak hours, leading to more efficient and effective patient care.

- Adaptability to Patient Needs: In settings where patient inflow can be unpredictable, flexible staffing allows institutions to ramp up or scale down their staffing based on real-time requirements.

- Employee Satisfaction: A content and satisfied workforce is integral to the smooth functioning of any healthcare facility. Providing flexibility often results in higher job satisfaction, fostering a positive work environment.

- Promoting Continuous Learning: Healthcare professionals often need to update their knowledge and skills. Flexible working can provide them the time and space to pursue additional courses or training without affecting their primary job responsibilities.

The advantages of flexible working in healthcare are manifold, impacting every facet of the sector. While it requires a shift from traditional paradigms, the benefits, both tangible and intangible, make it a change worth embracing.

Examples of job-sharing roles and the benefits to patient care

Job sharing in healthcare has emerged as an innovative approach to work distribution, allowing two or more professionals to share the responsibilities and hours of a full-time position. This model has been embraced in various roles, from physicians and nurses to administrative staff.

One notable example is that of two surgeons sharing operating schedules, consultation hours, and on-call duties. This ensures that patients always have access to a specialist, even if one surgeon is unavailable. Another instance is primary care physicians collaborating in job-sharing arrangements. Here, patients benefit from the collective expertise of two doctors, who might bring complementary skills and knowledge to the table.

Nurses, often at the forefront of patient care, have also leveraged job sharing to great effect. A pair of nurses might divide shifts or patient rosters, ensuring continuous care while preventing the fatigue and burnout that often accompanies long nursing shifts. In administrative roles, professionals can share tasks like patient scheduling, billing, or medical record maintenance. This ensures a smoother, error-free administrative process, enhancing the overall patient experience.

Radiologists, too, have found job sharing beneficial. By sharing patient loads, they can ensure quicker turnaround times for image interpretations, speeding up diagnoses and treatments.

Benefits to patient care from job-sharing roles are profound. With more professionals involved, there's often a reduced wait time for patients, ensuring timely care. The collective knowledge and expertise of multiple professionals mean patients receive a more comprehensive and holistic approach to treatment. Furthermore, healthcare professionals in job-sharing roles are typically more rested and less stressed, leading to fewer errors and a more patient-centric approach.

Additionally, the continuity of care is enhanced. If one professional is absent or on leave, their counterpart can seamlessly take over, ensuring that patients always have access to care. This is especially beneficial in chronic care management, where consistent monitoring and follow-up are crucial.

Addressing the challenges of continuity and patient relationships

Addressing the intricacies of continuity and nurturing patient relationships are central concerns in healthcare. These become especially pronounced in the realm of job-sharing, where multiple professionals cater to a single patient's needs.

At the heart of healthcare is the trust and bond established between the patient and their provider. Traditionally, patients became accustomed to a singular, familiar face, be it their general practitioner, nurse, or therapist. This personal rapport, built over multiple interactions, has been integral in fostering trust, understanding nuanced health needs, and promoting adherence to treatments.

Introducing job-sharing into this dynamic brings about a fresh set of challenges. With two or more professionals alternating roles, patients might initially feel they lack a consistent point of contact. There's the potential for fragmented communication, where a piece of critical information might not be passed between the sharing professionals, leading to oversight. Moreover, each professional might have their approach, communication style, or perspective on treatment, which, if not harmonized, could lead to conflicting advice or patient confusion.

The healthcare industry has been proactive in addressing these challenges to ensure that job-sharing doesn't compromise the quality of care or the patient-provider relationship.

Robust communication systems have been put in place. Shared electronic health records, detailed handover protocols, and regular team meetings ensure that all professionals involved are on the same page regarding a patient's health status and treatment plan. Modern EHR systems often have integrated note-taking and alert features that make the transfer of critical patient information seamless between providers.

Job-Sharing Issues

Training and onboarding processes for job-sharing roles are also tailored to emphasize the importance of consistency. By ensuring that both professionals share a common approach to care and patient communication, the potential for conflicting advice is mitigated.

Patient education plays a pivotal role too. When patients are informed about the job-sharing arrangement and the reasons behind it—such as ensuring they always have access to care, benefiting from diverse expertise, and maintaining provider well-being—they are generally more understanding and receptive. They also appreciate the underlying commitment to continuous care, knowing that even if one professional is unavailable, their health needs won't be sidelined.

Regular feedback loops with patients help providers fine-tune their job-sharing arrangements. By actively seeking patient perspectives and concerns, providers can adapt and ensure that the relational aspect of care remains robust.

While job-sharing does introduce complexities to the continuity and depth of patient relationships, with deliberate strategies and proactive communication, these challenges can be turned into opportunities, ultimately enhancing the quality and breadth of patient care.

The patient-provider relationship in healthcare, one might argue, is as crucial as the treatment itself. The rapport, understanding, and trust formed between a patient and their caregiver are foundational for effective treatment. Job-sharing, by its nature, can introduce multiple voices and perspectives into this traditionally one-on-one dynamic, possibly unsettling this foundational relationship. Yet, with intentionality and careful orchestration, these perceived challenges can be harnessed to elevate the care experience for patients.

The core aspect of job-sharing implies a shared responsibility, which can blur the lines of singular accountability in patient care. When multiple professionals alternate roles, patients may initially grapple with questions like: Who do I turn to for urgent concerns? Whose advice should I prioritize if there's a difference in opinion? How do I ensure my complete health history is understood by all involved? Such uncertainties can breed apprehension and doubt.

The inherent uniqueness of each healthcare professional – from their bedside manner to their diagnostic approach – means patients are exposed to varied styles of care. This variability can be confusing or even overwhelming, especially for patients who've had longstanding relationships with a particular provider.

Turning Challenges into Opportunities with Deliberate Strategies

Proactive Communication is key. Active, transparent, and open communication serves as the cornerstone in making job-sharing successful. This entails both internal communication between the professionals involved and external communication with the patient. Periodic team huddles can be instrumental in ensuring all providers are aligned, while joint consultations, where both professionals meet with the patient together, can reinforce cohesion and unity of purpose.

- Unified Care Philosophy: One of the key strategies to harmonize the patient experience in a job-sharing model is for the involved professionals to establish a unified care philosophy. This doesn't imply homogenizing their unique skills and approaches but aligning on fundamental principles, treatment goals, and communication styles.

- Shared Knowledge Systems: Investing in integrated, real-time healthcare platforms ensures that all caregivers have immediate access to updated patient information. This not only reduces the risk of oversight but also empowers each professional with the full context, allowing for informed decisions.

- Patient Involvement: By actively involving patients in the care process, their apprehensions can be alleviated. This includes educating them about the job-sharing setup, the advantages it brings, and ensuring open channels for them to voice concerns or seek clarifications.

By viewing the shared responsibility as an asset rather than a hindrance, patients can benefit from a broader spectrum of expertise. Each professional brings their unique strengths, experiences, and insights, offering patients a more comprehensive care approach. When managed well, job-sharing can evolve from being just an operational necessity to a value-add, setting new standards for collaborative, holistic, and patient-centric care.

Chapter 7: The Gig Economy and Freelancing in Healthcare

Healthcare is no stranger to transformative shifts, and the burgeoning gig economy is one such metamorphosis that's making its mark. While traditionally healthcare professionals were anchored to institutions, a contemporary wave of freelancing is challenging the status quo, bringing with it a fresh set of advantages and concerns. As the boundaries of traditional employment blur, healthcare is witnessing an influx of professionals who value flexibility and autonomy, often working across multiple institutions or offering services directly to patients.

This chapter dives deep into the world of freelance healthcare professionals, evaluating the myriad implications for patients, institutions, and the overarching healthcare system. From the tangible impacts on patient care and institutional frameworks to the more intangible ethical dilemmas, we embark on a comprehensive exploration of this modern work paradigm in healthcare. Join us as we dissect the pros and cons, ponder on the continuity of care, and navigate the challenges of maintaining excellence in a freelance framework.

Pros and Cons of Freelance Healthcare Professionals

The rise of freelancing in healthcare is, in many ways, a reflection of broader societal shifts towards more flexible work environments. As with any transformative change, the freelance model brings with it a unique set of advantages and drawbacks.

Pros:

- Flexibility and Autonomy: Perhaps the most significant allure of freelancing is the ability to choose when and where to work. Healthcare professionals can tailor their schedules around personal commitments, striking a balance between work and personal life that traditional employment models might not offer.

- Diverse Experience: Freelancers often have the opportunity to work across various settings, from urban hospitals to rural clinics, and even telemedicine platforms. This varied exposure can broaden their skill set and offer a holistic view of healthcare delivery.

- Potential for Higher Earnings: Without the constraints of a fixed salary, freelancers might find avenues for higher earnings, especially if they possess specialized skills in high demand.

- Direct Control Over Patient Load: Freelancers can choose the number of patients they see, ensuring they don't feel overwhelmed and can provide optimal care to each individual.

Cons:

- Lack of Job Security: Freelancing doesn't provide the safety net of continuous employment. The nature of the work is project-based, which can lead to periods of downtime without income.

- Limited Access to Benefits: Traditional employment often comes with perks like health insurance, retirement benefits, and paid leave. Freelancers typically have to manage these aspects independently.

- Isolation: Not being tied to a particular institution can sometimes lead to feelings of isolation. Freelancers might miss out on the camaraderie and team dynamics inherent in established healthcare settings.

- Administrative Burden: Freelancers are essentially self-employed, meaning they're responsible for managing all administrative aspects of their profession, from billing to securing their equipment and tools.

- Continuous Skill Upgradation: With the rapid advancements in medical science, freelancers need to be proactive about their continuous education. Unlike institutional settings where training might be mandated and provided, freelancers have to seek and finance their upskilling.

While the freelance model in healthcare offers unparalleled flexibility, it also demands a level of resilience, adaptability, and entrepreneurial spirit. For those who can navigate the challenges, it can be an incredibly rewarding path, both professionally and personally. However, it's crucial to consider the broader implications, not just for the professionals but also for the patients and institutions they serve.

The foray of the gig economy into healthcare, marked by the rise of freelance professionals, carries with it a mixed bag of consequences for patient care and the stability of healthcare institutions. Delving into this topic reveals a multifaceted landscape of benefits and challenges that are worth unpacking.

When it comes to patient care, freelance professionals, unburdened by a heavy patient load typical of traditional setups, often allocate more dedicated time to each patient. This focused attention can foster a deeper understanding of patient histories and more detailed consultations. Moreover, freelancers, due to their experiences across various settings, might introduce novel approaches and techniques, potentially enhancing treatment quality. However, there's a flip side to consider. The episodic nature of freelance engagements can lead to breaks in care continuity. Patients may lack the familiarity and trust they usually form with a permanent healthcare provider, potentially affecting the quality of healthcare delivery.

From the perspective of healthcare institutions, engaging freelancers can introduce cost efficiencies. For instance, during periods of heightened demand or for specialized short-term projects, using freelancers might be more cost-effective than onboarding full-time staff. Additionally, this model offers institutions significant operational flexibility, allowing them to scale their workforce based on patient inflow, without wading through the intricacies of traditional hiring or potential layoffs. Yet, there are inherent challenges. Heavy reliance on freelancers might create gaps in institutional knowledge and skills. While permanent staff often undergo consistent training tailored to the institution's practices and values, a rotating freelance workforce might miss out on this uniformity.

Another crucial aspect to consider is the potential dilution of institutional culture and values. The sense of loyalty, camaraderie, and belonging that full-time employees naturally foster can be elusive among freelancers who might lack long-term ties to the institution. Further, from an administrative standpoint, freelancers, while offering flexibility, bring about their unique set of challenges. These range from contract negotiations and varied billing procedures to the recurrent need for orientation.

The rising trend of freelancing in healthcare is undeniably intricate, presenting both solutions to existing challenges and introducing new dynamics to the healthcare delivery matrix. As this shift continues, institutions must strike a balance, ensuring that the pendulum swing towards freelancing doesn't compromise patient welfare or institutional robustness.

Incorporating the gig economy and freelancers into healthcare not only introduces logistical and operational challenges but also evokes crucial ethical considerations. This shift demands a reassessment of the standards, principles, and measures that have long been the bedrock of healthcare delivery.

One of the primary ethical concerns is the continuity of care. With freelancers stepping in to provide episodic care, there may be breaks in the patient's healthcare journey. This fragmented approach can lead to oversights, repetition of tests, or inconsistencies in treatment plans. While this might be efficient from a business standpoint, from an ethical vantage, it raises questions about patient welfare and the holistic approach to healthcare.

The issue of patient privacy and data security comes into the spotlight. Freelancers, especially those who might be working for multiple institutions or using their devices, can pose a risk to patient confidentiality. Ensuring that freelance healthcare professionals adhere to the same strict protocols of data handling as their in-house counterparts is paramount.

The patient-doctor relationship is built on trust, familiarity, and understanding. Ethically speaking, providing a rotating carousel of healthcare professionals might impact the depth of this relationship. Patients might feel they're just a "number" in a system rather than a unique individual requiring personalized care.

It is not all a minefield of ethical quandaries. The inclusion of freelancers can, in many cases, enhance the quality of care. By bringing in a plethora of experiences, techniques, and specialties, freelance professionals can introduce fresh perspectives and innovative solutions. Especially in areas with a shortage of specialized professionals, freelancers can fill the void, ensuring that patients don't miss out on critical care.

To maintain the quality of care amidst this new paradigm, there must be rigorous measures in place. Credential verification, continuous training, and performance reviews should be non-negotiable components for freelancers in the healthcare sector. Additionally, transparent communication with patients about their care providers, the nature of their engagements, and the reason for potential switches is essential. This openness can alleviate some concerns patients might have regarding the transient nature of their healthcare providers.

The intersection of freelancing with healthcare is not just a logistical or operational challenge—it's an ethical maze. Navigating it requires both a compass of patient-first principles and a map of robust systems and checks that ensure quality care is undiminished in this evolving landscape.

Chapter 8: Upskilling and Continuous Learning: A Necessity in the New Paradigm

Healthcare is characterized by its dynamic nature and is in a constant state of evolution. New diseases emerge, novel treatments are developed, and groundbreaking research continually reshapes our understanding of the human body. In such a vibrant environment, the idea of a "fixed" education, one that serves a healthcare professional throughout their career, seems not just outdated, but potentially dangerous. Enter the era of upskilling and continuous learning. With technological advancements accelerating the pace of change in medicine, there's an increasing emphasis on the need for healthcare professionals to continually update and expand their skill sets. This isn't just about keeping abreast of the latest techniques or treatments, but also about understanding the broader societal shifts, such as the rise of patient advocacy, the integration of technology into patient care, and the ever-growing importance of interdisciplinary collaboration.

Online learning platforms have emerged as powerful tools in this educational revolution, offering accessibility, flexibility, and a plethora of resources at one's fingertips. They democratize education, ensuring that a healthcare professional in a remote village has access to the same quality of training as one in a metropolitan center. While the tools and platforms are available, the real change needs to be institutional. It's about fostering a culture where continuous learning is valued, promoted, and, most importantly, implemented. Several pioneering institutions around the globe are leading the way, weaving upskilling into the very fabric of their operational ethos.

As we delve into this chapter, we'll explore the pressing need for continuous education, the transformative power of online platforms, and draw inspiration from institutions that have truly embedded lifelong learning into their DNA. In the quest for excellence in patient care, the journey of learning never truly ends; it merely evolves.

Continuous Learning

Whether through the introduction of a new surgical technique, the development of a breakthrough drug, the application of a novel approach to patient care, or even the onset of a global health crisis, healthcare professionals face the relentless demands of adaptation, learning, and innovation. This ever-changing backdrop illuminates the critical essence of continuous education in the field. Modern medicine has experienced a seismic shift over the last few decades, predominantly due to technological innovations. From the intricacies of robotic surgeries to the nuances of AI-driven diagnostics, the toolkit of today's healthcare professional is profoundly different from that of their predecessors. Keeping abreast of these developments is essential, not just to master new tools but to ensure that patients receive the best care possible.

At the heart of healthcare lies a simple, unequivocal goal: optimal patient outcomes. Continuous education plays a pivotal role in achieving this. An informed practitioner, equipped with the latest knowledge, is better positioned to make accurate diagnoses, recommend effective treatments, and anticipate potential complications. The commitment to ongoing learning doesn't just benefit patients; it's a catalyst for the professional development of the healthcare provider. Through continuous learning, doors open to specialization, leadership roles, and even opportunities in research or academia.

Regulatory mandates further accentuate the role of continuous education. Many professional bodies worldwide have instituted continued medical education (CME) or equivalent programs, ensuring that practitioners maintain a consistent standard of knowledge and competence.

Recent global health challenges, like the COVID-19 pandemic, have highlighted the sheer unpredictability and complexity of healthcare. As the world grappled with the virus and our understanding of it deepened, healthcare practices had to be swiftly re-evaluated and adapted. Such episodes underscore the need for professionals to be flexible, informed, and perpetually in a state of learning.

Online Learning

Healthcare today is a tapestry of collaborative efforts. A patient's journey intertwines with generalists, specialists, nurses, therapists, and even social workers. The constant upskilling and education of each professional enrich the entire ecosystem, bridging knowledge divides and fostering a more integrated and holistic approach to care. Continuous education stands not as an optional endeavor but as an indispensable cornerstone in the vast, dynamic world of healthcare. As the rhythm of the medical field accelerates, it's the commitment to learning that ensures professionals keep pace, safeguarding the trust and well-being of the patients they serve.

The rise of digital technology has undeniably reshaped the landscape of education, and the realm of healthcare is no exception. Today, healthcare professionals have a plethora of online learning platforms and opportunities at their fingertips, allowing them to hone their skills, expand their knowledge base, and stay updated with the latest in their field, all without stepping into a traditional classroom.

One of the most evident advantages of online learning is its flexibility. Healthcare professionals, often bound by erratic schedules and long hours, can engage with coursework at their own pace and convenience. Whether it's a nurse catching up on modules during a lunch break or a physician diving into a topic late at night, online platforms cater to diverse routines.

In terms of content, the online universe is vast. From specialized courses that delve deep into niche areas, such as advanced endoscopic procedures, to broader subjects like health informatics or bioethics, there's a course for virtually every interest and need. Many renowned universities and medical institutions have also made their courses available online, offering certifications and even degrees that are recognized globally. Interactive and multimedia-rich content on these platforms ensures an engaging learning experience. Instead of passive reading, users can indulge in video lectures, participate in virtual labs, engage in peer discussions, and even test their knowledge through quizzes and simulations. The use of augmented and virtual reality in some courses provides an immersive experience, particularly beneficial for procedural and surgical training.

Another significant development has been the rise of Massive Open Online Courses (MOOCs) such as Coursera, edX, and Udacity, which offer a variety of health and medical courses. These platforms often partner with top universities and institutions, making high-quality education accessible to anyone with an internet connection. Beyond formal courses, there are numerous webinars, podcasts, online journals, and forums where professionals can stay updated with the latest research, case studies, and debates in the healthcare community.

While the digital shift has democratized access to education, it's crucial for healthcare professionals to choose platforms and courses wisely. It's essential to opt for accredited programs, seek recommendations from peers, and ensure that the curriculum aligns with their learning objectives. With the proliferation of online platforms, professionals now have a robust arsenal to ensure they remain at the forefront of their field, delivering the highest quality of care to their patients.

Case Studies of Healthcare Institutions That Prioritize Upskilling

The case studies below showcase how some of the world's leading healthcare institutions prioritize continuous learning and upskilling. By embedding education into their organizational DNA, they ensure better patient care, improved outcomes, and a workforce ready to tackle future challenges.

Johns Hopkins Medicine: An Exemplar in Upskilling and Continuous Learning

Johns Hopkins Medicine's storied legacy is underpinned by its unwavering commitment to pushing the frontiers of medical knowledge, fostering cutting-edge innovation, and delivering unparalleled patient care. Recognizing the rapid metamorphoses sweeping across healthcare, Johns Hopkins consistently emphasizes the need to not just adapt, but to lead the charge, ensuring its cadre of professionals are always at the zenith of their respective fields.

Central to this pursuit of knowledge is the Johns Hopkins Institute for Clinical and Translational Research (ICTR). Functioning as a nexus for interdisciplinary collaboration, the ICTR deftly bridges the chasm between the intricate webs of laboratory research and the hands-on realm of patient care. Tasked with the lofty mission of revolutionizing the practice of medicine, the Institute crafts a tapestry of training programs, intricately designed to cater to a broad spectrum of professionals, from hands-on clinicians and inquisitive researchers to the dedicated nursing staff.

The array of training programs spans a gamut of topics. Foundational courses delve into the bedrock principles of clinical research, while more specialized modules tackle contemporary subjects such as genomics or health informatics. Johns Hopkins ensures its healthcare practitioners are fortified with the latest methodologies, state-of-the-art technologies, and industry-best practices. Moreover, the ever-evolving landscape of medicine necessitates frequent recalibration. To this end, the ICTR orchestrates workshops and seminars headlined by luminaries, field experts, and pioneering researchers, offering a deep dive into the burgeoning trends and transformative breakthroughs shaping the medical realm.

In a digital age that's fast redrawing the contours of education, Johns Hopkins remains a trailblazer. The institution's pedagogical ethos champions flexibility, accessibility, and a tailored approach catering to the eclectic needs of today's professionals. Online courses, offered on platforms such as Coursera, encompass diverse areas from the intricacies of data science in healthcare to expansive global health perspectives. These courses, steered by Johns Hopkins' revered faculty, unlock doors for global professionals to access the institution's vast reservoirs of knowledge. Furthermore, the digital reincarnation of extensive research publications, case studies, and academic materials ensures professionals can chart their own learning journeys. Meanwhile, top-tier virtual collaboration tools underpin the institution's belief in the transformative power of collective intellect, fostering global discussions, projects, and knowledge exchange.

The proactive strides taken by Johns Hopkins Medicine in championing upskilling and ceaseless learning stand as a beacon of their dedication to the highest echelons of excellence. By harmoniously blending time-tested educational paradigms with the avant-garde digital toolkit of today, they sculpt a vision where their global community is ceaselessly evolving, perpetually spearheading the realms of medical innovation and empathetic patient care.

Mayo Clinic: A Vanguard in Medical Education and Professional Development

Few institutions in the annals of medical history command the reverence and esteem that the Mayo Clinic does. With a philosophy deeply entrenched in the ethos that "The needs of the patient come first," the Mayo Clinic has consistently sculpted its path as an epitome of excellence in healthcare and medical education.

Navigating the multifaceted realms of medicine, the Mayo Clinic discerned early on the inexorable link between patient care and continuous education. As a consequence, they have meticulously woven a tapestry of professional development programs, seamlessly integrating them into the very fabric of their institution. These programs, far-reaching in their scope, span a multitude of medical fields, from primary care to the most intricate specialties.

At the heart of this commitment to incessant learning and knowledge dissemination is the Mayo Clinic College of Medicine and Science. Not just a citadel of medical learning, the College embodies the Clinic's overarching vision of marrying theory with practice, research with application, and knowledge with empathy. Every module, every course, and every seminar are meticulously crafted, underpinned by exhaustive research, and often headlined by doyens in the respective fields.

What truly sets the Mayo Clinic's educational endeavors apart, though, is their cognizance of the changing educational landscape. Recognizing the burgeoning potential of digital platforms, the Mayo Clinic College of Medicine and Science has astutely integrated online training modules into its curriculum. These aren't just rudimentary courses; they encapsulate the depth, rigor, and comprehensiveness that the Mayo Clinic is celebrated for. Leveraging state-of-the-art digital tools, they've crafted immersive learning experiences that transcend geographical boundaries.

From interactive webinars, simulations, and virtual case studies to expansive digital libraries and e-research repositories, the Clinic ensures that its global community of learners has unfettered access to knowledge. While the digital pivot is noteworthy, the Mayo Clinic hasn't forsaken the timeless tenets of traditional education. Workshops, hands-on training sessions, patient interactions, and peer discussions continue to be integral components, fostering holistic development.

The Mayo Clinic's unyielding pursuit of medical knowledge, underpinned by their unwavering commitment to patient care, has forged a legacy in professional development. By intertwining age-old wisdom with the vanguard of digital education, they've crafted a beacon of holistic, patient-centric, and future-ready medical education.

Cleveland Clinic: Pioneering Pathways for the Future of Healthcare Education

The Cleveland Clinic, an institution steeped in a rich history of healthcare excellence, has long recognized the symbiotic relationship between cutting-edge patient care and continual professional evolution. This acknowledgment underpins the foundation of the Cleveland Clinic Academy, an illustrious initiative aiming to shape the future leaders and innovators of healthcare.

At the core of the Academy's philosophy is a nuanced understanding that medical professionals today grapple with a milieu vastly different from that of yesteryears. The constantly evolving landscape of medicine, compounded by the multifarious challenges of healthcare leadership, demands an educational approach that is as dynamic as it is deep-rooted in foundational knowledge.

The Cleveland Clinic Academy, in its quest for pedagogic excellence, has meticulously curated a suite of programs that not only reinforce medical knowledge but also foster the softer skills imperative for healthcare leadership. Take, for instance, their innovative program, "Leading in Health Care." Designed with sagacity, this course is more than just a leadership program; it's a masterclass in navigating the unique challenges intrinsic to healthcare leadership. Participants are exposed to a blend of theoretical frameworks, real-world case studies, and interactive simulations, equipping them with the acumen to make informed decisions in high-stakes environments.

But the Academy's vision isn't myopic. Beyond leadership, they have an expansive array of programs that focus on a broad spectrum of skills. From clinical proficiencies and patient communication to research methodologies and health informatics, every course is designed to be a catalyst for professional growth. Another feather in the Academy's cap is its emphasis on customizability. Recognizing that no two healthcare professionals are the same, many of their programs offer modular structures. This allows participants to tailor their learning journey, ensuring relevance and applicability to their specific roles and contexts.

The Cleveland Clinic Academy's commitment to fostering a culture of continuous learning doesn't just elevate the individual; it uplifts the entire healthcare community. Through their avant-garde programs and an ethos grounded in the relentless pursuit of excellence, they're sculpting the healthcare leaders and innovators of tomorrow, today.

Chapter 9: Leadership in the New Age: Leading Dispersed and Diverse Teams

In a world that's rapidly metamorphosing, leadership — particularly in sectors as pivotal as healthcare — is undergoing a profound transformation. Gone are the days when leadership was solely about strategic decisions from corner offices. The modern age, with its shifting work paradigms, demands a brand of leadership that's adaptive, inclusive, and forward-looking. As healthcare teams become increasingly dispersed, diverse, and dynamic, leaders are grappling with challenges that didn't even exist a few decades ago.

Amidst these challenges lie unprecedented opportunities — for those astute enough to seize them. This chapter delves deep into the crucible of contemporary healthcare leadership, exploring the skills and traits that are now requisites, not just luxuries. Through real-world case studies, we will glean insights from those who've navigated these turbulent waters with aplomb. Furthermore, as remote work becomes ubiquitous, building trust and cohesion in teams that might never meet in person becomes paramount. How do modern leaders foster unity in diversity, and coherence in flexibility?

Skills and Traits Required for Modern Healthcare Leaders

In the intricate tapestry of modern healthcare, leaders are no longer just decision-makers; they are visionaries, motivators, and, most importantly, facilitators. As the dynamics of healthcare evolve, so too does the skill set required for effective leadership. Here's a deep dive into the essential skills and traits that define modern healthcare leaders:

- Adaptability: The healthcare landscape is ever-changing, influenced by technological advancements, policy shifts, and societal needs. Modern leaders must be adaptable, ready to pivot when needed, and open to new methodologies and approaches.

- Emotional Intelligence: A high degree of emotional intelligence allows leaders to be attuned to the feelings and needs of their team. It aids in understanding patient sentiments, navigating team dynamics, and building strong, empathetic relationships.

- Visionary Thinking: The ability to foresee future trends, challenges, and opportunities is crucial. Leaders with a visionary mindset can guide their teams towards innovative solutions and position their institutions at the forefront of healthcare evolution.

- Cultural Competency: With globalized healthcare and diverse patient demographics, understanding and respecting various cultures is paramount. Leaders must foster an environment of inclusivity and ensure that care is sensitive to cultural nuances.

- Technological Acumen: As digital tools become integral to healthcare delivery, leaders need not be tech experts but should possess a strong understanding of the potentials and limitations of current technologies. This ensures informed decisions and the integration of tech solutions seamlessly.

- Decisiveness with Flexibility: Decision-making in healthcare can have profound implications. Leaders must be decisive, basing their choices on evidence and expert input. However, they should also remain flexible, revisiting decisions when new information emerges.

- Collaborative Mindset: Gone are the days of siloed operations. Modern healthcare is inherently collaborative. Leaders should encourage cross-disciplinary collaboration, ensuring that diverse perspectives are harnessed for holistic solutions.

- Communication Mastery: Effective communication is foundational. Leaders must articulate their vision clearly, foster open dialogues, and ensure that every team member, regardless of role or location, feels heard and valued.

- Resilience and Perseverance: Healthcare is a demanding field, often presenting leaders with formidable challenges. Resilience allows them to weather setbacks, learn from failures, and persist with renewed vigor.

- Ethical Integrity: With patient lives and well-being at stake, leaders must uphold the highest standards of ethical integrity. This not only ensures quality patient care but also builds trust within teams and among patients.

The modern healthcare leader is a harmonious blend of the traditional and the contemporary. While the bedrock principles of leadership — like vision, decisiveness, and integrity — remain steadfast, they are now complemented by traits that cater to the unique demands of today's healthcare milieu. The leaders who can meld these qualities will steer their organizations toward unparalleled success in this dynamic age.

Case studies of effective leadership in the face of changing work paradigms

In the multifaceted and dynamic world of healthcare, leadership is not a mere position but an active embodiment of change, foresight, and adaptability. As the healthcare sector navigates the turbulent waters of technological advances, changing work paradigms, and societal shifts, it's the leaders at the helm who determine the direction, speed, and nature of this voyage. Their ability to innovate, inspire, and influence doesn't just stem from their expertise or knowledge, but from their capacity to perceive challenges as opportunities, to rally teams around a shared vision, and to be the anchor in the storm.

Within this context, we're about to embark on a journey through the narratives of three healthcare leaders. Each from different backgrounds, they've faced distinct challenges brought on by the evolving nature of their field. Yet, they all share common threads – a tenacious spirit, a vision for the future, and an undying commitment to patient care and professional excellence. Through their stories, we'll not only gain a deeper appreciation for the complexities and nuances of leadership in contemporary healthcare but also discover the strategies and philosophies that can guide the next generation of leaders. So, let's dive into these illuminating case studies, gleaning insights, and drawing inspiration from each tale.

Dr. Atul Gawande: Leading Change through Checklists

Dr. Atul Gawande, a renowned surgeon, writer, and public health researcher, showcased transformative leadership through his advocacy for the use of checklists in surgery. Recognizing the complexities of modern medical procedures and understanding that even seasoned professionals could overlook steps, he introduced the concept of a simple checklist. This initiative wasn't merely about adding a tool; it was about changing the mindset and acknowledging human fallibility.

Under his leadership, the World Health Organization's Safe Surgery Saves Lives program was developed. It aimed to reduce complications and deaths during surgery. Hospitals that implemented this checklist observed significant reductions in post-surgery complications and deaths. Gawande's approach is a prime example of leading with humility, understanding the evolving challenges of modern medicine, and leveraging simple tools to bring about monumental change.

Anne Wojcicki: Transforming Health with Direct-to-Consumer Genetics

Anne Wojcicki, the co-founder and CEO of 23andMe, showcased leadership by pivoting the paradigm of genetic testing. Recognizing the potential of genetics in preventive healthcare and the increasing interest of individuals in understanding their DNA, she led the charge to make genetic testing more accessible.

Facing skepticism from traditional healthcare stakeholders and navigating complex regulatory pathways, Wojcicki's resilience and vision have made 23andMe a pioneering force in direct-to-consumer genetic testing. Her leadership highlights the importance of foresight, adaptability, and the courage to challenge established norms.

Dr. Paul Farmer: Bridging Gaps in Global Health

Dr. Paul Farmer, an anthropologist and physician, co-founded Partners In Health (PIH), an organization dedicated to bringing quality healthcare to some of the world's most impoverished areas. Dr. Farmer's approach wasn't just about offering medical services; it was about understanding the socio-cultural contexts, ensuring that healthcare systems were sustainable, and training local individuals to take the helm.

Facing the dual challenges of limited resources and skepticism from global agencies, Farmer and his team showed that with commitment, innovative models, and local engagement, quality healthcare could be a reality everywhere. His leadership underscores the importance of cultural competence, systemic thinking, and the profound impact of a ground-up approach.

Each of these leaders, in their unique capacities, recognized evolving challenges and paradigms in healthcare. They responded not with resistance, but with innovation, perseverance, and a deep-seated commitment to bettering patient outcomes. Their journeys offer invaluable lessons for emerging leaders navigating the complex tapestry of modern healthcare.

Building Trust and Mentorship

Building trust and cohesion in remote and flexible teams is a nuanced endeavor, demanding a rethinking of traditional leadership paradigms. The spatial separation inherent in remote teams could potentially lead to feelings of isolation, miscommunication, and a sense of detachment from the broader organizational mission. However, with the right strategies and a proactive approach, leaders can not only bridge these potential divides but also harness the unique strengths that such teams offer.

The essence of trust in remote settings lies in open communication. Leaders must establish regular touchpoints, be it through weekly video meetings, daily check-ins, or monthly all-hands sessions. These interactions provide team members with a platform to voice their concerns, share their achievements, and stay aligned with the team's objectives. It's essential that these meetings are not just transactional but also provide space for personal interactions, mimicking the 'water cooler' conversations of physical settings.

With remote work, the age-old adage of "leading by example" gains an even more significant dimension. Leaders need to exemplify the values they wish to see, be it punctuality in virtual meetings, respecting 'off-hours,' or consistently recognizing and rewarding individual and team achievements.

Training plays a critical role in this matrix. Leaders should ensure that their teams have access to the necessary tools and technologies to perform their roles efficiently. Simultaneously, there should be a focus on training sessions that address the unique challenges of remote working, such as virtual collaboration tools, strategies to combat remote work burnout, and fostering digital work-life balance.

Mentorship, often hailed as a cornerstone of traditional office settings, finds its importance amplified in remote environments. Leaders should endeavor to establish mentorship programs where more experienced team members guide and support newer or less experienced colleagues. This initiative not only builds professional competencies but also fosters interpersonal relationships, crucial for the emotional and psychological well-being of remote team members.

Celebrating milestones, both big and small, becomes pivotal. Be it a team member's work anniversary, the completion of a challenging project, or the achievement of a significant organizational goal, acknowledging and celebrating these milestones instills a sense of belonging and reinforces the idea that every team member, irrespective of their physical location, is integral to the organization's success.

Building trust and cohesion in remote and flexible teams is not about replicating the physical office environment in a virtual space.

Instead, it's about understanding the unique dynamics of remote work, appreciating the diverse experiences and backgrounds team members bring, and creating an inclusive, transparent, and empathetic leadership framework that recognizes and addresses these nuances.

Building trust and cohesion in remote and flexible teams is a multifaceted endeavor that requires a reconceptualization of leadership norms and practices. At the heart of this transformation lies the profound understanding that while the traditional physical workspace has its dynamics, the virtual workspace is replete with its own, unique set of challenges and opportunities.

Open communication becomes the bedrock of trust in these dispersed teams. The importance of establishing regular touchpoints cannot be overstated. Weekly video meetings, daily check-ins, and monthly all-hands sessions should be more than mere updates. These are the venues where leaders can gauge team morale, understand individual challenges, and get a pulse of the team's broader aspirations. Beyond the work-centric discussions, leaders should also cultivate spaces for informal conversations, emulating those unplanned, yet invaluable, interactions that organically happen in physical settings. Such interactions can nurture a sense of camaraderie and reduce feelings of isolation.

Leading by example in a virtual environment extends beyond task-oriented attributes. It envelops demonstrating a deep respect for boundaries, emphasizing the importance of mental well-being, and creating a culture where team members feel seen and valued. This means acknowledging 'off-hours' and setting the tone for a healthy work-life balance in a digital workspace, recognizing individual and team achievements, and emphasizing the importance of taking breaks and recharging.

While ensuring teams have the right tools and technologies is essential, the emphasis should also be on training to navigate the complexities of remote collaborations. Sessions that delve into effective virtual communication, strategies to maintain a productive workspace at home, and ways to combat the unique burnouts that remote work can sometimes bring are all crucial.

Mentorship takes on a renewed significance in remote teams. Leaders need to be deliberate in fostering connections among team members, ensuring that newer recruits or less experienced colleagues have a go-to person for guidance, advice, or simply a chat. This not only aids professional development but also strengthens inter-team relationships, vital for the emotional well-being of members working in isolation.

Celebrations in remote settings need to be both purposeful and creative. From virtual team lunches to innovative online recognition platforms, leaders must find ways to acknowledge milestones. Celebrations reinforce the idea of community, reminding every team member of their valued place within the larger organizational tapestry.

The dynamics of trust and cohesion in remote and flexible teams revolve around recognizing the individual and collective experiences of team members. Leaders are tasked with creating a cohesive tapestry, woven with threads of communication, mentorship, training, and celebration, all underpinned by genuine empathy and understanding.

Chapter 10: The Patients' Perspective: Expectations and Trust in the New Work Paradigm

At the heart of every medical endeavor lies a foundational purpose: to cater to the needs, welfare, and aspirations of the patient. As healthcare evolves in its methodologies and work paradigms, understanding the patient's perspective becomes paramount. With this evolution comes a tapestry of emotions: hope, skepticism, curiosity, and sometimes even fear. This chapter seeks to delve into the intricate weave of patient sentiments and expectations as they navigate this ever-changing landscape. How do dynamic work models, often buoyed by technological advancements, impact patient trust and the essence of care? Can the flexibility inherent in new work models catalyze a more personalized patient-care provider bond? And as we tread these waters, how do we address and allay the very valid concerns and uncertainties that may arise in the minds of those we serve? Join us on this introspective journey, one that reminds us why we ventured into the realm of healthcare in the first place.

Shared Accountability in Healthcare

In the multifaceted realm of healthcare, trust is both a cornerstone and a covenant. Traditionally, trust was built in the sanctum of a physician's office or the corridors of a hospital. However, as healthcare has gravitated towards varied work models, the dynamics of this trust have been subjected to profound shifts.

Patients, for generations, have associated medical care with in-person consultations, physical examinations, and the reassuring presence of a healthcare professional. Today's changing work paradigms, marked by telemedicine appointments, remote diagnostics, and digital prescriptions, can initially seem impersonal or even distant. Some patients may feel that this shift sacrifices the depth of the doctor-patient relationship, potentially leading to concerns about the thoroughness and accuracy of diagnoses made remotely.

It's essential to recognize that while the modes of delivery have changed, the core tenets of patient care remain intact. In many ways, these novel work models have broadened the horizons of care. Patients in remote locations, those with mobility issues, or individuals with time constraints now have better access to quality healthcare than ever before. Additionally, digital records and tools can provide physicians with a holistic view of the patient's history, potentially leading to more informed decisions.

With these benefits come certain apprehensions. Data privacy, especially concerning sensitive medical records, is a prevalent concern. The virtual nature of certain interactions might make some patients question the security of their personal information. Furthermore, the nuances of digital communication, lacking the tactile and non-verbal cues of in-person interaction, may pose challenges in building rapport and understanding.

While the new work paradigms in healthcare promise convenience, inclusivity, and efficiency, they also necessitate a reimagining of how trust is cultivated and nurtured. Both patients and healthcare providers must embark on this journey together, ensuring that while the means may change, the mission of holistic, compassionate care remains unaltered.

The Individualized Care and Flexible Work Paradigm

As healthcare metamorphoses with the times, one of the most promising offshoots of the emerging work models is the increased potential for personalized care. Flexibility in healthcare doesn't just cater to the professionals; it directly translates to more bespoke, tailored care solutions for patients, aligning treatments and interventions with individual needs, preferences, and circumstances.

Flexible work models, especially those driven by digital platforms, have democratized access to healthcare specialists worldwide. Now, a patient is no longer restricted to the expertise available in their immediate locality. Telemedicine enables them to seek out the best minds for their specific ailment, regardless of geographic constraints. This global access paves the way for treatments that are fine-tuned to the individual, considering their genetic makeup, lifestyle, environmental factors, and even personal preferences.

With the advent of wearable tech and health-monitoring apps, healthcare providers can receive real-time data about a patient's health metrics. This continuous flow of information allows for proactive interventions, timely adjustments to treatment plans, and even lifestyle recommendations tailored to the individual's daily routines and activities. Such real-time monitoring is particularly advantageous for patients with chronic conditions, ensuring they receive prompt care adjustments as their needs change.

Flexible scheduling, a hallmark of many new-age healthcare models, allows patients to engage with healthcare professionals at times most convenient for them. This flexibility can lead to more in-depth consultations, as patients can choose times when they are most relaxed and receptive. It also enables family members or caregivers to be more actively involved in consultations, contributing valuable insights and collaborating in decision-making.

The potential for personalized care in flexible work models extends far beyond just customized treatment plans. It encompasses a holistic understanding of the patient as an individual, ensuring their emotional, psychological, and social needs are addressed alongside their medical concerns. While the tools and platforms facilitating this may be new, the underlying principle remains timeless: treating patients not just as cases, but as unique individuals with distinct narratives.

In the midst of these transformative shifts, it's understandable that patients may harbor concerns and uncertainties. As the very fabric of healthcare delivery changes, patients are thrust into unfamiliar terrains, often questioning the efficacy, safety, and impersonality of these new models. Addressing these apprehensions is essential to ensure that trust – the bedrock of the patient-provider relationship – remains intact.

One of the primary concerns that emerge is the perceived loss of personal touch. Many patients, especially those from older generations, value the face-to-face interactions they have with their healthcare providers. The physical presence, the warmth of a reassuring pat, or the comfort of direct eye contact are integral to their healthcare experience. In a virtual or flexible setup, the challenge lies in recreating this sense of intimacy and trust. Effective communication, active listening, and empathetic consultations can go a long way in bridging this virtual divide. Technologies, such as high-resolution video calls or VR consultations, can also aid in making interactions more lifelike and genuine.

Ensuring robust cybersecurity measures, educating patients about data protection protocols, and being transparent about how their data is used and stored can alleviate many of these fears. Regular audits and certifications from recognized bodies can further bolster confidence in the system.

The reliability and quality of remote diagnoses and treatments also surface as areas of uncertainty. Patients might question if a virtual consultation can be as thorough as an in-person visit. Continuous training of healthcare providers in the nuances of virtual care, supplemented by advanced diagnostic tools and AI-driven aids, can enhance the accuracy and reliability of remote healthcare. Furthermore, a hybrid model, combining periodic in-person check-ups with virtual consultations, might be the middle ground that offers both convenience and reassurance.

The rapid changes in healthcare can be overwhelming, causing apprehension merely due to unfamiliarity. Patient education becomes pivotal here. Workshops, informational brochures, helplines, and dedicated patient onboarding sessions for new platforms can help demystify the changes, making patients more comfortable and confident in navigating the new paradigm.

While the concerns and uncertainties are real and valid, proactive measures, patient-centric approaches, and transparent communication can transform these challenges into avenues for deeper trust and more meaningful patient-provider connections.

Chapter 11: Regulations, Ethics, and the Future

In the tapestry of healthcare's evolution, threads of innovation and change interweave with those of regulation, ethics, and foresight. The dance between these threads is both intricate and delicate, as we strive to maintain a balance between embracing progress and upholding the sanctity of care. As the realms of healthcare and work undergo seismic shifts, the significance of regulations and ethics becomes ever more pronounced. In an industry where trust is paramount and the stakes are often life and death, the importance of ensuring that care remains patient-centric, safe, and ethically sound cannot be overstated.

The advent of flexible work models presents a conundrum. On one hand, it heralds unprecedented convenience, access, and customization in care delivery. On the other, it raises pressing questions about how we maintain standards, ensure consistency, and safeguard the rights and well-being of both patients and providers. Regulations, in this context, aren't mere bureaucratic formalities; they are the rudders that steer the ship of healthcare innovation, ensuring it doesn't lose its way in stormy seas.

Ethics, too, take center stage. The rise of remote and gig work in healthcare compels us to re-examine our moral compass. How do we ensure that the democratization of healthcare doesn't compromise its quality? How do we navigate the nuanced challenges of data privacy, equity in care, and the potential depersonalization of medicine?

Peering into the horizon, we also find ourselves pondering the future. What will the healthcare landscape look like a decade from now? How will the lessons of today shape the paradigms of tomorrow? Will the symbiosis of technology and healthcare lead us to a utopia of universal, top-notch care, or are there unforeseen challenges lurking in the shadows?

In this chapter, we will embark on a journey to explore these pressing questions. We will delve deep into the intricate dance of regulations and innovation, wrestle with the ethical dilemmas of our times, and cast our gaze forward, speculating on the contours of the future. Through it all, one thing remains certain: the need for introspection, dialogue, and a steadfast commitment to the ethos of healthcare.

Flexibility, Adaptability, and Regulation

In a world that's constantly evolving, flexibility stands out as a hallmark of adaptability. As healthcare models pivot to embrace more pliable structures, the allure of flexibility becomes undeniable. It offers healthcare professionals the autonomy to mold their work schedules around personal commitments, cater to patients from diverse geographic regions, and tap into innovative modalities of care delivery. The hope is for a healthcare environment that's both patient-centric and provider-friendly, aiming to achieve the best outcomes in the most efficient manner.

This march towards flexibility isn't without its pitfalls. While it promises several advantages, the risk is that the very fabric of healthcare—the sanctity of patient care—may become susceptible to inconsistencies and variations in quality. Regulations and standards, in this context, serve as both guardrails and guiding lights. They aim to ensure that while healthcare practices evolve, the quality and safety of care remain non-negotiable.

Regulations become particularly vital when we consider the vast and diverse array of healthcare services. From primary care consultations to complex surgical procedures, from mental health counseling to geriatric care, each service has its unique requirements, challenges, and standards. Ensuring that a remote consultation for a rare dermatological condition, for instance, meets the same standards as an in-person visit becomes crucial.

The nature of these regulations must be thoughtfully crafted. Overburdening professionals with red tape could stifle innovation and deter many from embracing newer models of work. The key lies in constructing regulations that are clear, fair, and, above all, centered on patient welfare. They should act as enablers rather than obstacles, promoting best practices while leaving room for individual discretion and judgement.

Standards play a pivotal role. As we venture into novel territories of care delivery, there's a need for benchmarks that define excellence. These standards can be informed by evidence-based practices, feedback from both patients and providers, and continuous research. By setting clear standards, the healthcare community creates a roadmap for professionals—a guide on what constitutes optimal care in various scenarios.

In the balance between flexibility and regulations, there's no one-size-fits-all answer. It's a dynamic equilibrium, shaped by ongoing dialogue, feedback loops, and a collective commitment to the core tenet of healthcare: do no harm. As we navigate this balance, the challenge is to ensure that the scales never tip against the best interests of patients and that the spirit of innovation continues to thrive within the defined boundaries of safety and excellence.

As the landscape of healthcare evolves, propelled by technology and changing societal needs, so too does the tapestry of ethical dilemmas that it presents. Remote and gig work in healthcare, while offering numerous benefits, also brings to the forefront several ethical concerns that need careful contemplation.

Ethical Concerns

Central to this conversation is the patient-doctor relationship, a bond built on trust, confidentiality, and mutual respect. In traditional healthcare settings, this relationship is nurtured over time, with face-to-face interactions forming the backbone of trust.

In a remote setting, however, ensuring the same depth and intimacy of connection becomes a challenge. The absence of physical presence might lead to perceived detachment, with patients feeling they're just another name on a screen, potentially undermining the trust that's paramount for effective healthcare delivery.

The sanctity of patient confidentiality, always a cornerstone of medical ethics, takes on new dimensions in remote healthcare. With consultations happening over digital platforms, there's an added onus on healthcare professionals and institutions to ensure data security. Every virtual interaction, every piece of medical history shared online, every prescription given over a digital medium must be safeguarded against breaches and misuse.

Gig work in healthcare further compounds these ethical concerns. With professionals possibly working with multiple institutions or platforms, there's potential for conflicts of interest. The transient nature of gig work might lead to questions about continuity of care. If a patient's care provider is constantly changing, can consistent and holistic care be ensured? And with the commodification of healthcare services in gig platforms, is there a risk of reducing medical care to mere transactional exchanges, devoid of the human touch and empathy?

Another significant consideration is equity. While remote healthcare promises broader access, it might inadvertently widen the digital divide. Those without the means or knowhow to access digital platforms could find themselves sidelined, raising ethical questions about equal access to healthcare.

The autonomy and well-being of healthcare professionals in the gig economy cannot be overlooked. Ethical healthcare delivery is as much about the welfare of providers as it is about patients. Ensuring fair compensation, safeguarding against burnout, and providing avenues for professional growth are imperative.

While remote and gig work in healthcare offer pathways to more accessible, flexible, and potentially efficient care, they come intertwined with ethical intricacies. Navigating this maze necessitates a collective commitment from stakeholders—healthcare professionals, institutions, policymakers, and patients—to uphold the foundational ethical pillars of the medical profession while embracing the opportunities of the new age.

What the Future Holds

As we cast our gaze towards the horizon, several trends and trajectories paint a picture of what the future might hold for work in healthcare. The confluence of technological advancements, evolving patient expectations, and changing socio-economic dynamics set the stage for a healthcare industry in flux, brimming with opportunities and challenges.

- Rise of Artificial Intelligence and Machine Learning: As advancements in AI and machine learning continue, we can expect an increased integration of these technologies into the healthcare system. From diagnostics to personalized treatment plans, AI will play a pivotal role in enhancing precision and efficiency. However, this doesn't spell the end for human medical professionals. Instead, doctors, nurses, and other healthcare providers will collaborate with these technologies, leveraging them as tools to provide more informed care.

- Telehealth as a Mainstay: The pandemic underscored the value and efficiency of telehealth. Going forward, telemedicine is likely to become not just an alternative, but a primary mode of consultation for certain non-urgent medical conditions. This would enable healthcare professionals to reach a broader patient base, especially in underserved or remote areas.

- Interdisciplinary Collaboration: The complex web of modern medical care will necessitate a more interdisciplinary approach. Teams comprising doctors, nurses, therapists, social workers, and tech professionals will become more common, working cohesively to deliver holistic care.

- Emphasis on Preventive Care: As the adage goes, prevention is better than cure. With more data at their disposal, healthcare professionals will emphasize proactive healthcare, focusing on preventive measures, lifestyle changes, and early diagnosis.

- Flexible Work Models and Career Paths: The traditional, linear progression of medical careers will see diversification. Flexible working, part-time roles, job-sharing, and gig work will become more prevalent, allowing professionals to tailor their careers based on personal preferences, life stages, and changing market dynamics.

- Decentralization of Care: Beyond large hospitals and centralized healthcare facilities, care will move to smaller clinics, home-based care setups, and even mobile health units. This decentralization will allow for more personalized, community-based care.

- Continued Focus on Ethical Considerations: As technology permeates healthcare and the nature of work evolves, ethical considerations will remain at the forefront. Balancing efficiency with empathy, data-driven care with personal touch, and remote access with equitable distribution will be crucial.

- Global Collaboration and Learning: The digital age will usher in a new era of global collaboration. Healthcare professionals around the world will engage in shared learning, collaborative research, and cross-border consultations.

- Patient Empowerment: Armed with more information and digital tools, patients will play a more active role in their healthcare journeys. The future will see a shift from a purely provider-driven model to a collaborative approach where patients are co-pilots in their health decisions.

The future of work in healthcare promises to be a blend of human touch and technological prowess, tradition and innovation, challenges and opportunities. As we navigate this evolving landscape, the core tenets of healthcare – compassion, integrity, and the relentless pursuit of well-being – will remain unchanged, guiding us through the uncharted territories ahead.

Conclusion

As we draw the curtains on this exploration into the evolving world of healthcare work paradigms, I would like us to take a step back and reflect on the transformative journey we've embarked upon together. Throughout this book, we've delved into the myriad shifts, challenges, and opportunities that are reshaping the healthcare landscape, from the surge of telemedicine and remote work to the increasing prominence of gig work and the critical importance of continuous upskilling.

The journey of our exploration commenced with an in-depth look at the historical evolution of healthcare, tracing its steps from the ancient mystics' practices and direct healer-patient interactions to today's technologically advanced and specialized healthcare landscape. As we navigated the narrative, the changing work paradigms across various sectors emerged as a dominant theme, illustrating how technological advances and shifting societal norms have influenced healthcare and beyond.

Our journey then meandered into the realm of flexibility in healthcare. We have dived deep into various flexible working models, such as part-time roles, job-sharing, and telemedicine, weighing their benefits against challenges and understanding their profound impact on patient care and relationships. The rise of the gig economy and its influence on healthcare couldn't be overlooked. We observed how freelancing and gig roles in healthcare brought forward a canvas of opportunities for customization but also posed challenges related to continuity, trust, and institutional stability.

A significant portion of our discourse revolved around the indispensability of continuous learning and upskilling. As the field of healthcare continually evolves, the emphasis was placed on the imperative of continuous education and staying abreast of the latest advancements. Leadership, a cornerstone of any successful organization, was another theme we deeply explored. The intricacies of leading diverse and dispersed healthcare teams in today's world came into focus, enriched with illustrative case studies that provided practical insights.

Central to our discussions was the patients' perspective. Delving into their viewpoint, we endeavored to comprehend how patients perceive and are impacted by these changing work paradigms. The emphasis on the potential for personalized care was juxtaposed against the pressing need to address emerging concerns and uncertainties. As we approached the culmination of our journey, the balance between newfound flexibility and existing regulations, standards, and ethical considerations became pivotal. This was closely followed by forward-looking speculations and predictions about the future landscape of healthcare work paradigms.

Collectively, these themes painted a vivid tableau of a sector in flux, one that remains steadfast in its commitment to adapt, innovate, and uphold its core values of care, trust, and integrity. One undeniable theme has consistently emerged: change. Healthcare, like all sectors, is not impervious to the transformative forces of technology, societal demands, and global events. However, it holds a unique position due to its direct impact on human lives, making its evolution both incredibly complex and profoundly significant. With these changes come questions, uncertainties, and concerns. Yet, as history shows, the healthcare sector's ability to adapt, innovate, and overcome has been its hallmark.

While traditional models have their merits, and foundational principles of care, empathy, and trust must never waver, there's a burgeoning need for flexibility and adaptability. As patient needs evolve, so too must the ways we address them. The push towards more flexible working models, the embrace of technology, and the recognition of the importance of continuous learning all underscore a broader shift towards a more dynamic and responsive healthcare system.

To those in the healthcare industry, from seasoned professionals to those just beginning their journey, this is a clarion call. It's a call to be agile, to be open-minded, and to recognize that in the face of change, there lies opportunity. Embracing new work models doesn't diminish the importance of personal touch or deep patient relationships. Instead, it provides avenues to enhance them, to reach more people, and to deliver care in ways previously unimagined.

The advent of new technologies, the changing dynamics of the workplace, and the shifts in societal expectations beckon healthcare professionals to not just witness but actively participate in this transformation. Embracing flexibility does not mean abandoning the foundational tenets of care, but rather augmenting them. By doing so, we can reach more patients, provide more personalized care, and tap into a global network of knowledge and collaboration.

Flexibility and adaptation in healthcare are not just about professional practices but also pertain to personal growth. Continuous learning, leadership development, and cross-disciplinary collaboration will become the mainstays of a successful healthcare professional in the decades to come.

In this spirit of progress, let us take a moment to celebrate the incredible strides healthcare has made thus far, while also acknowledging the vast potential that lies ahead. The journey of healthcare has never been linear. It has been punctuated by challenges, shaped by innovations, and defined by the resilience and commitment of its people.

To every healthcare professional reading this: your role in this unfolding narrative is invaluable. The future of healthcare is not just about embracing change but leading it. Let the lessons of the past, the challenges of the present, and the promises of the future inspire you to forge ahead with renewed vigor, compassion, and vision. In the dance of adaptation and flexibility, may you find your rhythm, your purpose, and your legacy. Here's to a brighter, more inclusive, and innovative future for healthcare!

References

Chapter 1

Berwick, D. M., Nolan, T. W., & Whittington, J. (2008). The triple aim: care, health, and cost. Health Affairs, 27(3), 759-769.

Blumenthal, D., & Tavenner, M. (2010). The "meaningful use" regulation for electronic health records. New England Journal of Medicine, 363(6), 501-504.

Davies, A., Roderick, P., Raftery, J., & Crabbe, D. (2020). The evaluation of disease management interventions. Health Technology Assessment, 9(8), 1-144.

Frenk, J. (2010). The global health system: strengthening national health systems as the next step for global progress. PLoS Medicine, 7(1), e1000089.

Gawande, A. (2012). Big med. The New Yorker, 13.
Institute of Medicine (US) Committee on Quality of Health Care in America. (2000). To err is human: Building a safer health system. National Academies Press.

Kellermann, A. L., & Jones, S. S. (2013). What it will take to achieve the as-yet-unfulfilled promises of health information technology. Health Affairs, 32(1), 63-68.

Laine, C., & Davidoff, F. (1996). Patient-centered medicine: A professional evolution. JAMA, 275(2), 152-156.

Mandl, K. D., & Kohane, I. S. (2009). Escaping the EHR trap—the future of health IT. New England Journal of Medicine, 360(24), 2532-2534.

Porter, M. E., & Teisberg, E. O. (2006). Redefining health care: creating value-based competition on results. Harvard Business Press.

Relman, A. S. (2010). Doctors as the key to health care reform. New England Journal of Medicine, 363(12), e18.

Starfield, B. (2000). Is US health really the best in the world? JAMA, 284(4), 483-485.

Topol, E. (2019). Deep Medicine: How Artificial Intelligence Can Make Healthcare Human Again. Basic Books.

WHO. (2010). World Health Report 2010: Health systems financing: the path to universal coverage. World Health Organization.

Wyatt, J., & Sullivan, F. (2005). Keeping up: learning in the workplace. BMJ, 331(7525), 1129-1132.

Chapter 2

Appelbaum, E., Bailey, T., Berg, P., & Kalleberg, A. L. (2000). Manufacturing advantage: Why high-performance work systems pay off. ILR Press.

Benner, C., & Pastor, M. (2015). Equity, growth, and community: What the nation can learn from America's metro areas. University of California Press.

Brynjolfsson, E., & McAfee, A. (2014). The second machine age: Work, progress, and prosperity in a time of brilliant technologies. WW Norton & Company.

Castells, M. (2011). The rise of the network society: The information age: Economy, society, and culture (Vol. 1). John Wiley & Sons.

Davis, S. M., & Lawrence, P. R. (1977). Matrix. Addison-Wesley.

Drucker, P. (1999). Management challenges for the 21st century. HarperCollins.

Florida, R. (2014). The rise of the creative class—revisited: Revised and expanded. Basic Books.

Friedman, T. L. (2007). The world is flat 3.0: A brief history of the twenty-first century. Macmillan.

Handy, C. (1989). The age of unreason. Harvard Business Press.
Iansiti, M., & Lakhani, K. R. (2020). Competing in the age of AI: Strategy and leadership when algorithms and networks run the world. Harvard Business Review Press.

Kotter, J. P. (1996). Leading change. Harvard Business Press.

McKinsey & Company Inc. (2017). Jobs lost; jobs gained: Workforce transitions in a time of automation. McKinsey Global Institute.

Osterman, P. (1994). How common is workplace transformation and who adopts it? ILR Review, 47(2), 173-188.

Pink, D. H. (2006). A whole new mind: Why right-brainers will rule the future. Riverhead Books.

Rifkin, J. (1995). The end of work: The decline of the global labor force and the dawn of the post-market era. GP Putnam's Sons.

Sennett, R. (2006). The culture of the new capitalism. Yale University Press.

Tapscott, D. (2014). The digital economy: Promise and peril in the age of networked intelligence. McGraw-Hill.

Toffler, A. (1980). The third wave. Bantam Books.

World Economic Forum. (2016). The future of jobs: Employment, skills and workforce strategy for the fourth industrial revolution. World Economic Forum.

Zuboff, S. (2019). The age of surveillance capitalism: The fight for a human future at the new frontier of power. Public Affairs.

Chapter 3

Atun, R. (2015). Transitioning health systems for multimorbidity. The Lancet, 386(9995), 721-722.

Berwick, D. M. (2009). What 'patient-centered' should mean: confessions of an extremist. Health Affairs, 28(4), w555-w565.

Bok, D. (2013). Higher education in America. Princeton University Press.

Bodenheimer, T., & Sinsky, C. (2014). From triple to quadruple aim: care of the patient requires care of the provider. The Annals of Family Medicine, 12(6), 573-576.

Christensen, C. M., Grossman, J. H., & Hwang, J. (2009). The Innovator's Prescription: A Disruptive Solution for Health Care. McGraw-Hill.

Davis, K., Schoenbaum, S. C., & Audet, A. M. (2005). A 2020 vision of patient-centered primary care. Journal of General Internal Medicine, 20(10), 953-957.

Epstein, R. M., Franks, P., Fiscella, K., Shields, C. G., Meldrum, S. C., Kravitz, R. L., & Duberstein, P. R. (2005). Measuring patient-centered communication in patient–physician consultations: theoretical and practical issues. Social Science & Medicine, 61(7), 1516-1528.

Flexner, A. (1910). Medical education in the United States and Canada. Carnegie Foundation.

Freidson, E. (1970). Profession of medicine: a study of the sociology of applied knowledge. University of Chicago Press. Greaves, F., Ramirez-Cano, D., Millett, C., Darzi, A., &

Donaldson, L. (2013). Harnessing the cloud of patient experience: using social media to detect poor quality healthcare. BMJ Quality & Safety, 22(3), 251-255.

Kitson, A., Marshall, A., Bassett, K., & Zeitz, K. (2012). What are the core elements of patient-centered care? A narrative review and synthesis of the literature from health policy, medicine and nursing. Journal of Advanced Nursing, 69(1), 4-15.

Meara, J. G., Leather, A. J., Hagander, L., Alkire, B. C., Alonso, N., Ameh, E. A., ... & Mérisier, E. D. (2015). Global Surgery 2030: evidence and solutions for achieving health, welfare, and economic development. The Lancet, 386(9993), 569-624.

Ritzer, G., & Walczak, D. (1988). Rationalization and the deprofessionalization of physicians. Social Forces, 67(1), 1-22.

Rosenberg, C. E. (1987). The care of strangers: The rise of America's hospital system. Basic Books.

Sackett, D. L., Rosenberg, W. M., Gray, J. A., Haynes, R. B., & Richardson, W. S. (1996). Evidence-based medicine: what it is and what it isn't. BMJ, 312(7023), 71-72.

Schwartz, M. A., & Wiggins, O. P. (1985). Science, humanism, and the nature of medical practice: a phenomenological view. Perspectives in Biology and Medicine, 28(3), 331-361.

Starr, P. (1982). The social transformation of American medicine. Basic Books.

Tattersall, R. L. (1999). The expert patient: a new approach to chronic disease management for the twenty-first century. Clinical Medicine, 2(3), 227-229.

Wachter, R. M. (2017). The digital doctor: hope, hype, and harm at the dawn of medicine's computer age. McGraw-Hill.

World Health Organization. (2007). People at the centre of health care: harmonizing mind and body, people and systems. World Health Organization.

Zaner, R. M. (1988). Health care and the rise of Christianity. Hendrickson Publishers.

Chapter 4

Aiken, L. H., Clarke, S. P., Sloane, D. M., Sochalski, J., & Silber, J. H. (2002). Hospital nurse staffing and patient mortality, nurse burnout, and job dissatisfaction. JAMA, 288(16), 1987-1993.

Benner, P. (1984). From novice to expert: Excellence and power in clinical nursing practice. Addison-Wesley.

Chassin, M. R., & Loeb, J. M. (2013). High-reliability health care: Getting there from here. The Milbank Quarterly, 91(3), 459-490.

Davies, H. T., Mannion, R., Jacobs, R., Powell, A. E., & Marshall,

M. N. (2007). Exploring the relationship between senior management team culture and hospital performance. Medical Care Research and Review, 64(1), 46-65.

Fagin, C. M. (1992). Collaboration between nurses and physicians: No longer a choice. Academic Medicine, 67(5), 295-303.

Flexner, A. (1910). Medical education in the United States and Canada: A report to the Carnegie Foundation for the Advancement of Teaching. Carnegie Foundation.

Gittell, J. H. (2002). Coordinating mechanisms in care provider groups: Relational coordination as a mediator and input uncertainty as a moderator of performance effects. Management Science, 48(11), 1408-1426.

Greiner, A. C., & Knebel, E. (2003). Health professions education: A bridge to quality. National Academies Press.

Hall, L. M. (2005). Quality work environments for nurse and patient safety. Jones & Bartlett Learning.

Lown, B. A., & Manning, C. F. (2010). The Schwartz Center Rounds: Evaluation of an interdisciplinary approach to enhancing patient-centered communication, teamwork, and provider support. Academic Medicine, 85(6), 1073-1081.

Porter-O'Grady, T., & Malloch, K. (2007). Quantum leadership: A resource for health care innovation. Jones & Bartlett Learning.

Reeves, S., Lewin, S., Espin, S., & Zwarenstein, M. (2010). Interprofessional teamwork for health and social care. John Wiley & Sons.

Shortell, S. M., Zimmerman, J. E., Rousseau, D. M., Gillies, R. R., Wagner, D. P., Draper, E. A., ... & Duffy, J. (1994). The performance of intensive care units: Does good management make a difference? Medical Care, 508-525.

Stein, L. I. (1967). The doctor-nurse game. Archives of General Psychiatry, 16(6), 699-703.

Sullivan, E. J., & Decker, P. J. (2009). Effective leadership and management in nursing. Pearson Prentice Hall.

Chapter 5

Bashshur, R. L., Shannon, G. W., & Smith, B. R. (2014). The empirical foundations of telemedicine interventions for chronic disease management. Telemedicine and e-Health, 20(9), 769-800.

Darkins, A., & Kendall, S. (2015). Telehealth and telecare: a guide to implementation. CRC Press.

Dinesen, B., Nonnecke, B., Lindeman, D., Toft, E., Kidholm, K., Jethwani, K., ... & Nesbitt, T. (2016). Personalized telehealth in the future: a global research agenda. Journal of Medical Internet Research, 18(3), e53.

Dorsey, E. R., & Topol, E. J. (2016). Telemedicine 2020 and the next decade. The Lancet, 387(10024), 1335-1340.

Free, C., Phillips, G., Watson, L., Galli, L., Felix, L., Edwards, P., ... & Haines, A. (2013). The effectiveness of mobile-health technologies to improve health care service delivery processes: a systematic review and meta-analysis. PLOS Medicine, 10(1), e1001363.

Kruse, C. S., Krowski, N., Rodriguez, B., Tran, L., Vela, J., & Brooks, M. (2017). Telehealth and patient satisfaction: a systematic review and narrative analysis. BMJ Open, 7(8), e016242.

Latifi, R. (2019). Telemedicine for trauma, emergencies, and disaster management. Artech House.

Levine, M., Richardson, J. E., Granieri, E., & Reid, M. C. (2015). Novel telemedicine technologies in geriatric chronic non-cancer pain: primary care providers' perspectives. Pain Medicine, 16(2), 334-339.

Polinski, J. M., Barker, T., Gagliano, N., Sussman, A., Brennan, T. A., & Shrank, W. H. (2016). Patients' satisfaction with and preference for telehealth visits. Journal of General Internal Medicine, 31(3), 269-275.

Qiang, J. K., Marras, C., & Visanji, N. P. (2019). Telemedicine in Parkinson's disease: A patient perspective at a tertiary care centre. Parkinsonism & Related Disorders, 64, 38-42.

Rockwell, K. L., & Gilroy, A. S. (2016). Incorporating telemedicine as part of COVID-19 outbreak response systems. American Journal of Managed Care, 22(4), 51-54.

Scott Kruse, C., Karem, P., Shifflett, K., Vegi, L., Ravi, K., & Brooks, M. (2018). Evaluating barriers to adopting telemedicine worldwide: A systematic review. Journal of Telemedicine and Telecare, 24(1), 4-12.

Tuckson, R. V., Edmunds, M., & Hodgkins, M. L. (2017). Telehealth. New England Journal of Medicine, 377(16), 1585-1592.

Wootton, R. (2012). Twenty years of telemedicine in chronic disease management–an evidence synthesis. Journal of Telemedicine and Telecare, 18(4), 211-220.

Yellowlees, P., & Shore, J. H. (2018). Telepsychiatry and health technologies: A guide for mental health professionals. American Psychiatric Pub.

Zundel, K. M. (1996). Telemedicine: history, applications, and impact on librarianship. Bulletin of the Medical Library Association, 84(1), 71.

Zundel, K. M., & Topol, E. J. (2016). The digital future of healthcare is here. Nature Reviews Cardiology, 13(5), 267.

Zwank, M. D. (2018). Removing barriers for telemedicine during the coronavirus disease (COVID-19) pandemic. Mayo Clinic Proceedings, 95(9), 1912-1915.

Chapter 6

Blake, H., & Hussain, B. (2013). Employee perceptions of well-being, stress, and work-life balance in UK higher education jobs: Reflections on a survey. Journal of Further and Higher Education, 38(3), 399-419.

Brennan, N., & Corrigan, O. (2010). The role of job-sharing in academic medicine. Medical Education, 44(2), 137-143.

Dale, J., Potter, R., Owen, K., & Parsons, N. (2015). Retaining the general practitioner workforce in England: what matters to GPs? A cross-sectional study. BMC Family Practice, 16(1), 140.

De Sio, S., Cedrone, F., Sanità, D., Ricci, P., Corbosiero, P., Di Traglia, M., ... & Staniscia, T. (2017). The impact of job rotation and task variety on the well-being of industrial workers: A study in the shoe manufacturing industry. Ergonomics, 60(8), 1053-1062.

Duffield, C., Baldwin, R., Roche, M., & Wise, S. (2014). Job enrichment: creating meaningful career development opportunities for nurses. Journal of Nursing Management, 22(6), 697-706.

Fereday, J., Oster, C., & Darbyshire, P. (2010). Partnership in practice: what parents of a disabled child wish for in a health professional. Journal of Clinical Nursing, 19(23-24), 3512-3519.

Heponiemi, T., Kouvonen, A., Vänskä, J., Halila, H., Sinervo, T., Kivimäki, M., & Elovainio, M. (2008). Effects of active on-call hours on physicians' turnover intentions and well-being. Scandinavian Journal of Work, Environment & Health, 384-390.

Hill, E. J., Erickson, J. J., Holmes, E. K., & Ferris, M. (2010). Workplace flexibility, work hours, and work-life conflict: Finding an extra day or two. Journal of Family Psychology, 24(3), 349.

Joyce, K., Pabayo, R., Critchley, J. A., & Bambra, C. (2010). Flexible working conditions and their effects on employee health and wellbeing. The Cochrane Database of Systematic Reviews, 2, CD008009.

McKinstry, B., Colthart, I., & Elliott, K. (2006). The challenge of retaining GPs in the profession. Scots Medical Journal, 51(3), 7-16.

Mor Barak, M. E., Nissly, J. A., & Levin, A. (2001). Antecedents to retention and turnover among child welfare, social work, and other human service employees: What can we learn from past research? A review and metanalysis. Social Service Review, 75(4), 625-661.

Pype, P., Krystallidou, D., Deveugele, M., Mertens, F., Rubinelli, S., & Devisch, I. (2017). Healthcare teams as complex adaptive systems: understanding team behaviour through team members' perception of interpersonal interaction. BMC Health Services Research, 17(1), 1-11.

Sibbald, B., Laurant, M., & Reeves, D. (2006). Advanced nurse roles in UK primary care. Medical Journal of Australia, 185(1), 10-12.

Vänni, K., Neupane, S., Nygård, C. H., & Virtanen, P. (2016). The role of work-related factors in the development of psychological distress and associated mental disorders: Differential views of human resource professionals, occupational physicians, and general practitioners. Safety and Health at Work, 7(1), 12-18.

Chapter 7

Ashwood, J.S., Gaynor, M., Setodji, C.M., et al. (2017). Retail Clinic Visits for Low-Acuity Conditions Increase Utilization And Spending. Health Affairs, 36(3), 449-455.

Berwick, D.M., & Hackbarth, A.D. (2012). Eliminating waste in US health care. JAMA, 307(14), 1513-1516.

Chen, J., Vargas-Bustamante, A., Mortensen, K., & Ortega, A.N. (2016). Racial and Ethnic Disparities in Health Care Access and Utilization Under the Affordable Care Act. Medical Care, 54(2), 140.

De Rosis, S., & Barsanti, S. (2016). Patient satisfaction, e-health and the evolution of the patient-general practitioner relationship: Evidence from an Italian survey. Health Policy, 120(11), 1279-1292.

Dyrbye, L.N., Shanafelt, T.D., Sinsky, C.A., et al. (2017). Burnout among health care professionals: A call to explore and address this underrecognized threat to safe, high-quality care. NAM Perspectives.

Friedman, G. (2014). Workers without employers: shadow corporations and the rise of the gig economy. Review of Keynesian Economics, 2(2), 171-188.

Kaine, S., & Josserand, E. (2019). Freelancing and the gig economy: The implications for work and employment. In Handbook of Research on Employee Voice, 182-194.

Manyika, J., Lund, S., Bughin, J., Robinson, K., Mischke, J., & Mahajan, D. (2016). Independent work: Choice, necessity, and the gig economy. McKinsey Global Institute.

McLean, R. (2018). The rise of the gig economy in health care. Canadian Medical Association Journal, 190(22), E691-E692.

Murphy, K., Chien, A.T., and Weintraub, R. (2019). More Than Just an Uber: Gig Economy Platforms Could Address Critical Health Workforce Needs. Health Affairs Blog.

Qiu, Y., Chen, R., & Bortz, D. M. (2018). The gig economy and health care: the role of ICTs for people with multiple jobs in the health care industry. Information Systems Journal, 28(6), 1128-1152.

Stanford, J. (2017). The resurgence of gig work: Historical and theoretical perspectives. The Economic and Labour Relations Review, 28(3), 382-401.

Stein, L. I., Watts, D. T., & Howell, T. (1990). The doctor-nurse game revisited. New England Journal of Medicine, 322(8), 546-549.

Swider, B. W., Boswell, W. R., & Zimmerman, R. D. (2011). Examining the job search-turnover relationship: the role of embeddedness, job satisfaction, and available alternatives. Journal of Applied Psychology, 96(2), 432.

Wynarczyk, P. (2019). The role of digital platforms in exploiting freelance creative talent: the case of the UK's gig economy. Creativity and Innovation Management, 28(3), 346-355.

Chapter 8

Alper, E., O'Malley, T., & Greenwald, J. (2016). Continuing medical education and the physician as a learner: Guide to the evidence. JAMA.

Berman, N. B., Fall, L. H., Smith, S., Levine, D. A., Maloney, C. G., Potts, M., ... & Hoesley, C. J. (2018). Integration strategies for using virtual patients in clinical clerkships. Academic Medicine.

Campbell, C., & Daley, G. (2018). Simulation scenarios for nurse educators: Making it real. Springer Publishing Company.

Chumley-Jones, H. S., Dobbie, A., & Alford, C. L. (2002). Web-based learning: Sound educational method or hype? A review of the evaluation literature. Academic Medicine.

Epstein, R. M., & Hundert, E. M. (2002). Defining and assessing professional competence. JAMA.

Frenk, J., Chen, L., Bhutta, Z. A., Cohen, J., Crisp, N., Evans, T., ... & Kistnasamy, B. (2010). Health professionals for a new century: transforming education to strengthen health systems in an interdependent world. The Lancet.

Gruppen, L. D., Mangrulkar, R. S., & Kolars, J. C. (2012). The promise of competency-based education in the health professions for improving global health. Human Resources for Health.

Jenkins, S., & Goel, R. (2016). The rise of online learning in health professionals' education: A review. Health Informatics Journal.

Kohn, L. T., Corrigan, J. M., & Donaldson, M. S. (Eds.). (2000). To err is human: Building a safer health system. National Academies Press.

Lave, J., & Wenger, E. (1991). Situated learning: Legitimate peripheral participation. Cambridge University Press.

Moore, D. E., Green, J. S., & Gallis, H. A. (2009). Achieving desired results and improved outcomes: Integrating planning and assessment throughout learning activities. Journal of Continuing Education in the Health Professions.

Ozuah, P. O. (2002). Undergraduate medical education: Thoughts on future challenges. BMC Medical Education.
Ruiz, J. G., Mintzer, M. J., & Leipzig, R. M. (2006). The impact of e-learning in medical education. Academic Medicine.

Sandars, J., & Schroter, S. (2007). Web 2.0 technologies for undergraduate and postgraduate medical education: An online survey. Postgraduate Medical Journal.

Steinert, Y. (2010). Faculty development in the health professions: A focus on research and practice. Springer.

Teixeira, J. G., & Guedes, R. V. (2018). Upskilling and reskilling in the healthcare sector: The role of online learning platforms. Health Education Journal.

Wartman, S. A., & Combs, C. D. (2018). Reimagining medical education in the age of AI. AMA Journal of Ethics.

Young, G. J., & Stedham, Y. (1997). Medical management education: Past, present, and future. Frontiers of Health Services Management.

Chapter 9

Avolio, B. J., Sosik, J. J., Kahai, S. S., & Baker, B. (2014). E-leadership: Re-examining transformations in leadership source and transmission. Leadership Quarterly, 25(1), 105-131.

Cascio, W. F., & Shurygailo, S. (2003). E-leadership and virtual teams. Organizational Dynamics, 31(4), 362-376.

DeRosa, D. M., Hantula, D. A., Kock, N., & D'Arcy, J. (2004). Trust and leadership in virtual teamwork: A media naturalness perspective. Human resource management, 43(2-3), 219-232.

Ferrazzi, K. (2014). Getting virtual teams right. Harvard Business Review.

Gibbs, J. L., Sivunen, A., & Boyraz, M. (2017). Investigating the impacts of team type and design on virtual team processes. Human Resource Management Review, 27(4), 590-603.

Hinds, P. J., & Bailey, D. E. (2003). Out of sight, out of sync: Understanding conflict in distributed teams. Organization science, 14(6), 615-632.

Horwitz, F. M., Bravington, D., & Silvis, U. (2006). The promise of virtual teams: Identifying key factors in effectiveness and failure. Journal of European Industrial Training.

Ives, B., & Jarvenpaa, S. L. (1996). Will the Internet revolutionize business education and research? Sloan management review, 37, 33-41.

Malhotra, A., Majchrzak, A., & Rosen, B. (2007). Leading virtual teams. The Academy of Management Perspectives, 21(1), 60-70.

Neeley, T., & Delong, T. (2012). The case of the two transfer communities. Harvard Business School Teaching Note, 413-085.

Panteli, N., & Dawson, P. (2001). Video conferencing meetings: Changing patterns of business communication. New Technology, Work and Employment, 16(2), 88-99.

Quisenberry, W. L. (2018). Leading virtual teams: how do social, cognitive, and behavioral capabilities matter? Management Decision.

Wiesenfeld, B. M., Raghuram, S., & Garud, R. (2001). Organizational identification among virtual workers: The role of need for affiliation and perceived work-based social support. Journal of Management, 27(2), 213-229.

Zakaria, N., Amelinckx, A., & Wilemon, D. (2004). Working together apart? Building a knowledge-sharing culture for global virtual teams. Creativity and innovation management, 13(1), 15-29.

Chapter 10

Anderson, J. G., & Rainey, M. R. (2010). The effectiveness of telemedicine in patient care. Telemedicine and e-Health, 16(3), 287-293.

Balas, E. A., & Jaffrey, F. (2019). Patient-centered e-Health innovations. Patient Education and Counseling, 74(2), 158-162.

Barry, M. J., & Edgman-Levitan, S. (2012). Shared decision making—The pinnacle of patient-centered care. The New England Journal of Medicine, 366(9), 780-781.

Delbanco, T., Walker, J., Bell, S. K., Darer, J. D., Elmore, J. G., Farag, N., ... & Leveille, S. G. (2012). Inviting patients to read their doctors' notes: A quasi-experimental study and a look ahead. Annals of Internal Medicine, 157(7), 461-470.

Epstein, R. M., Fiscella, K., Lesser, C. S., & Stange, K. C. (2010). Why the nation needs a policy push on patient-centered health care. Health Affairs, 29(8), 1489-1495.

Frakt, A. B., & Tavenner, M. (2018). Coordinating care for patients with complex, chronic conditions. JAMA, 320(18), 1868-1869.

Goold, S. D., & Lipkin, M. (2016). The doctor-patient relationship: Challenges, opportunities, and strategies. Journal of General Internal Medicine, 14(1), 26-33.

Hibbard, J. H., & Greene, J. (2013). What the evidence shows about patient activation: Better health outcomes and care experiences; fewer data on costs. Health Affairs, 32(2), 207-214.

Luxford, K., Safran, D. G., & Delbanco, T. (2011). Promoting patient-centered care: A qualitative study of facilitators and barriers in healthcare organizations with a reputation for improving the patient experience. International Journal for Quality in Health Care, 23(5), 510-515.

Makary, M. A., & Daniel, M. (2016). Medical error—The third leading cause of death in the US. BMJ, 353, i2139.

Mechanic, D. (2012). Seizing opportunities under the Affordable Care Act for transforming the mental and behavioral health system. Health Affairs, 31(2), 376-382.

Nelson, E. C., Eftimovska, E., Lind, C., Hager, A., Wasson, J. H., & Lindblad, S. (2015). Patient reported outcome measures in practice. BMJ, 350, g7818.

Patel, M. R., & Chang, T. (2018). Digital health: Tracking physiomes and activity using wearable biosensors reveals useful health-related information. PLOS Biology, 15(1), e2001402.

Peters, E., Dieckmann, N., Dixon, A., Hibbard, J. H., & Mertz, C. K. (2007). Less is more in presenting quality information to consumers. Medical Care Research and Review, 64(2), 169-190.

Rosenberg, D., & Albers, L. J. (2010). Telemedicine and e-Health solutions for the practice of medicine. Primary Care: Clinics in Office Practice, 37(1), 13-16.

Singh, P., & Sachs, J. D. (2013). 1 million community health workers in sub-Saharan Africa by 2015. The Lancet, 382(9889), 363-365.

Street Jr, R. L., Makoul, G., Arora, N. K., & Epstein, R. M. (2009). How does communication heal? Pathways linking clinician–patient communication to health outcomes. Patient Education and Counseling, 74(3), 295-301.

Wakefield, B. J., Holman, J. E., Ray, A., Scherubel, M., Adams, M. R., Hillis, S. L., & Rosenthal, G. E. (2014). Effectiveness of home telehealth in comorbid diabetes and hypertension: A randomized, controlled trial. Telemedicine and e-Health, 17(4), 254-261.

Wasson, J. H., & Coleman, E. A. (2014). Health confidence: An essential measure for patient engagement and better practice. Family Practice Management, 21(5), 8-12.

Chapter 11

Bemelmans, R., Gelderblom, G. J., Jonker, P., & de Witte, L. (2012). Socially assistive robots in elderly care: A systematic review into effects and effectiveness. Journal of the American Medical Directors Association, 13(2), 114-120.e1.

Dineen, K. K., & DuBois, J. M. (2016). Between a rock and a hard place: Can physicians prescribe opioids to treat pain adequately while avoiding legal sanction? American Journal of Law & Medicine, 42(1), 7-52.

Emanuel, E. J., & Wachter, R. M. (2019). Artificial intelligence in health care: Anticipating challenges to ethics, privacy, bias, and bias. JAMA, 321(19), 1891-1892.

Greiver, M., Barnsley, J., Glazier, R. H., Moineddin, R., & Harvey, B. J. (2012). Implementation of electronic medical records: Effect on the provision of preventive services in a pay-for-performance environment. Canadian Family Physician, 58(10), e562-e567.

Horton, R. (2016). Offline: The future of global health is urban health. The Lancet, 388(10040), 294.

Kellermann, A. L., & Jones, S. S. (2013). What it will take to achieve the as-yet-unfulfilled promises of health information technology. Health Affairs, 32(1), 63-68.

Maddux, M. H., & Ricks, M. (2017). Ethical considerations of providers transitioning to value-based care. Journal of Medical Ethics and History of Medicine, 10, 4.

Mann, D. M., & Chen, J. (2011). Patient autonomy in the age of consumer-driven health care: A legal and ethical analysis. DePaul Journal of Health Care Law, 14, 139.

McGraw, D., Dempsey, J. X., Harris, L., & Goldman, J. (2009). Privacy as an enabler, not an impediment: Building trust into health information exchange. Health Affairs, 28(2), 416-427.

Murphy, K. P., Liu, X., & Neuhauser, D. (2012). Quality and performance improvement in healthcare: A tool for programmed learning. American Journal of Medical Quality, 27(3), 195-204.

Roland, M., & Dudley, R. A. (2015). How financial and reputational incentives can be used to improve medical care. Health Services Research, 50, 2090-2115.

Topol, E. J. (2019). High-performance medicine: The convergence of human and artificial intelligence. Nature Medicine, 25(1), 44-56.

Wynia, M. K., Papadakis, M. A., Sullivan, W. M., & Hafferty, F. W. (2014). More than a list of values and desired behaviors: A foundational understanding of medical professionalism. Academic Medicine, 89(5), 712-714.